Her
and
Her

JANE MCKEARS

For Annette

Les and Edith – 1952 7

Joyce and Sylvia – 1962 17

Jenny and Diane – 1974 27

Penny and Hazel – 1978 39

Katy and Bronwen – 1988 53

Pippa and Kim – 1992 69

Claire and Gina – 1997 79

Cheryl and Anne – 2001 95

Edith and Mary – 2003 III

Les and Edith — 1952

The three of them were sitting in the Old Moseley Arms. They had in their right hands a pint of stout with a good head on it. In their left hands, they held a half-smoked Woodbine. They wore similar brown flat caps with fading checked patterns. And matching hob-nailed boots. Each wore a warm jacket which had been patched at the elbows.

A flickering small fire in the grate produced pungent smoke, and cast flashes of light across the room. The mantlepiece above held a framed photo of the recently-crowned queen. There were several stubs of used candles, congealing over their ceramic holders, a pile of spent matches, and someone's ration book. Upon the wall ticked a large oak clock, whose hourly chimes could be heard about the voices of the drinkers.

Eric, Phil and Les had started this tradition soon after the end of the war, to celebrate Hitler's death. Seven years later, the Friday night ritual continued. After work, they each walked to their own houses, and ate the meal their wives had prepared. They handed over their unopened wage packets. After stuffing their half-a-crown beer money into their trouser pockets, they strolled to the nearby pub.

Les was unusually quiet that night. Stroking his chin, shifting his position in the chair, and repeatedly looking out into the dark night. Heavy rain beat against the window, and he watched as it streamed down the glass. The wind was howling, and blowing the trees about, across the road. Some of the boughs looked as if they would snap in the storm. With his boot, he kicked the grit and crisp packets, which were spread across the chequered floor. Then he waved away the seafood man, saying that he couldn't face his usual Friday night pack of cockles.

Emptying his glass, he banged it onto the table like an auctioneer's gavel.

'Women!' he said. 'They drive you up the sodding wall.'

'Never a truer word spoke,' replied Phil, 'Damned if I can fathom 'em.'

Eric shook his head slowly from side to side. 'What some of them need is a bloody good hiding.'

'Violet's always going on about how hard it is, doing the washing in the dolly tub,' said Phil. 'I'll be damned if she knows what hard work is.'

'Aye,' said Eric. 'I can't imagine your Vi wheeling barrows of cement across the ruddy building site all day. They've no idea.'

And the three of them stared into the fire again, pondering on this. The coals smouldered, and grey smoke infiltrated the room.

'My round, I think,' said Les, carrying the empty glasses to the bar to be re-filled. He tossed his empty fag packet into the fire and a flame shot up.

Ivy had worked there as a bar maid for a few years. Since her Ken had been shot down in the war, she longed for company. And she needed the cash. She had worked in the ammunitions factory during the war, but now those men who had made it home, needed their jobs back. And she was happy enough at the pub. Only ten minutes' walk from her house, and she enjoyed the company of men.

'What can I get you darling?' she asked Les. Her wide smile exposing red lipstick on her teeth.

Les leaned forward and peered down her cleavage and chuckled.

'I'll make do with a Guinness for now,' he winked, and leaned his elbow on the bar.

'Cheeky boy,' whispered Ivy, with a grin.

Les carried the three pints across to his mates, smiling as he imagined having a quickie with Ivy. She wouldn't forget a night with him in a hurry!

Phil got out the dominoes, as he always did with the second pint. But Les's mind was elsewhere. After work that day, when he'd mopped up the last of the gravy from his whale meat stew, he was shocked to see Edith put a brand-new teapot on the table. Brand spanking new. Edith had bought their usual one only ten years earlier, when they had moved to Birming-ham to live together. A brand-new start.

'What the bloody hell is this?' he asked.

Edith's mouth twitched. She had got it as a bar-gain on the market that afternoon. A terracotta pot, much cheaper than the metal ones. The spout on the old one had broken. Chipped on the tap when she was emptying the tea leaves down the sink. Had cashed in the co-op divi. And she needed a decent pot for when the neighbours popped in for a cuppa. She gently placed the old knitted tea cosy on top of the new teapot, and smoothed it down.

'Why didn't you just get a rubber spout to stick on the old one?' he shouted. 'You were supposed to be saving the divi for Christmas. What we going to buy the chicken with now?'. Pulling on his jacket, he rushed down the hall, and slammed the door behind him.

Edith sat in front of the dying fire for a while. She looked around the room at all the things Les had done for them. Hanging the mirror above the fire. Filling the coal scuttle every night. Always bought a bunch of daffies on her birthday. And he'd never raised his hand to her. But still, he had no right to yell at her like that.

And now Les sat in his familiar watering hole, and mulled it over. Edith didn't often splash out like that and she knew they needed to watch the pennies. Even though they had no kids, things hadn't been easy for them. Moving towns in the middle of the war, to live where no-one knew them. Eking out the rations. They had rented a little terraced house in Moseley, which was handy for work at the foundry, and within walking distance of the pub. After all these years, Les still loved going home, to his little bit of privacy. And to his woman, Edith.

Edith had suggested she should go out to work again, after the war. Perhaps just a few hours at the corner shop, but Les wouldn't hear of it. Wouldn't let anyone say that he couldn't support his own wife. She'd stopped work as soon as the Jerries surrendered.

More than enough on her plate with looking after him and the house.

Eric ordered their third and last pint of the evening, disappointed that he didn't get the same jaunty smile from Ivy that she had lavished on Les. As always, they finished the night with a game of darts. Phil had the advantage, with being tallest, so his arms could reach the board more easily. Long shanks, they had called him, when he was younger. Easily climbed over the orchard walls to scrump apples. But Les showed the greatest precision, after years working as a welder. Had an eye for detail. And Eric was the most powerful, having built up his muscles as a labourer, on the railways. Les's darts shot across the room, hitting the bull's eye. Bullets from a gun.

Ivy moved towards the group, her high heels clicking on the flag-stoned floor. Five, four, three, two, one. Her skirt was tight, and her stocking seams were straight. She leaned over the adjacent table to collect the glasses. There was a waft of her perfume; Youth dew. Les glanced at the smooth, taut bum, and the pert boobs in the uplift bra. And when Ivy looked at him, with her head cocked to one side, he imagined fondling her.

'Later?' she whispered to Les.

'You kidding, Bab? The wife'd kill me,' he laughed, shaking his head.

So, he downed his drink, and bid the lads a good night. And forgot to wave to Ivy as he left. As he sauntered home. Les wondered what his mates would do if they ever guessed his secret after all these years. Found out that he was, in fact, a woman? Would they still want to spend their Friday nights together? Would dominoes and darts be different if they knew? But they would never know. Why would they? It had gone on so long that he rarely thought about it now. Living as a man, so that he could love his woman.

But as he walked along the unlit side roads, Les couldn't forget about the bloke in Rotherham, who had been murdered a couple of years ago, simply for walking down the street dressed as a woman. And he looked over his shoulder, cautiously. Was that chap following him? His heart beat quickened, and he felt sweat on his forehead. He stopped and looked in the corner shop window, then bent down as though to tie his shoelace. As the man walked past, calling out a cheery 'Goodnight, mate,' Les let out a long sigh.

When he approached his front door, he noticed how carefully the entry step had been scrubbed, and how proudly the brass door knob had been polished. The neat gingham curtains hanging in the front window. He cleaned his shoes on the boot scraper and stepped from the street into the red tiled hall. Les glanced at the framed photo of him and Edith, taken when they moved in there. Two determined faces, smiling at each other. Edith had gone without so much to live with him. And risked so much. Loyal and loving. There were no other photos, of course. No photos of the parents who had disowned them. No photos of children.

Les walked through to the kitchen. Edith was washing the saucepans, and the window was steamed up. Her mouth was pursed, and her flowery pinafore was still tied in place. She kept her back to Les as she cleaned the draining board. Then she wrung out the dish cloth and threw it hard, into the sink.

'Sorry, lass,' he grunted into her hair. 'I shouldn't have gone on like that.'

And he stroked her shoulder, and kissed the side of her neck, until she finally turned round to him.

'Come here, you miserable bugger,' she said, putting her arms around him.

And they stood together, quietly, for a moment. Each pressing their faces into the shoulder of the other. Les tugged her curls, and she stroked his face. They breathed rhythmically, in and out in time with each other.

Then Edith damped down the fire, while Les checked that the back door was locked.

As he walked up the stairs behind her, Les put his hand up Edith's skirt and undid her suspender. She shrieked and slapped his hand.

They writhed on the bed, and gave each other pleasure. Sweating. Gasping and moaning. The ice on the inside of the bedroom window began to thaw.

'You're a cantankerous old sod,' whispered Edith, 'But you're my man.'

'Well stop chucking my bloody money about then,' laughed Les.

And he climbed on top of Edith again, and gently parted her legs.

Joyce and Sylvia — 1962

'It's him,' said Sylvia, peering round the edge of the curtain into the street.

She could see Dennis from number 26, standing on their doorstep. Sighing she walked slowly towards the door.

'Just tell him to clear off,' called Joyce. 'You're too soft.'

The door opened, and in he sailed. He was tall, and seemed to use up a lot of room in their parlour. Without being asked, he flopped into the armchair that Sylvia had just vacated, leaving her to sit on a dining chair.

'Thought I'd drop in to see you ladies, as you're all alone,' he beamed. 'Thought you'd be glad of some company, with still being new to Birmingham.'

While Sylvia went to make the tea. Dennis and Joyce exchanged stares. He noticed that she had let herself go. No makeup. Shabby trousers. And her hair couldn't have seen a roller in years. A shame that a woman in her 30s wasn't trying to make the most of herself.

She noticed that he had polished his shoes recently, and was wearing an overpowering after-shave. Tabac? It reminded her of her uncle Eric, who had the good taste to use it sparingly. Dennis sat with his legs spread too wide, and his hands of the arms of the chair. His index finger scratched the edge of the chair arm, as he glanced towards the kitchen.

Sylvia carried the tray into the sitting room, and placed it on the coffee table, watched by Joyce and Dennis. A pretty, slender woman, in a gingham dress, and a cross-back apron. She handed each a tea plate and encouraged them to have a slice of angel cake. She straightened the tray cloth, which she had embroidered with flowers. Bright purple, and sunny yellow. Smiling as she poured the tea, she handed them both a cup, with a matching saucer. She and Joyce raised their little fingers, as they lifted their cups to drink.

Sylvia held eye contact with Joyce and tipped her head to one side. She wanted to meet the neighbours. Her old friends were all in Nottingham. Before they moved here, she had enjoyed spending time with them. She and Mary used to go to the pictures on a

Friday night. And she and Beryl went once a month to Jeff Wise's dance hall. That was where she met Joyce; what a turn-up for the books!

'Any jobs you ladies want doing, just let me know,' said Dennis. 'It's lovely having new neighbours but it must be hard for a couple of spinsters to be living alone like this.'

And he grinned into his tea cup. Sylvia suppressed a chuckle. Joyce crossed and uncrossed her legs and stared at the ceiling.

'You seem to work some odd shifts, Dennis' said Joyce. 'What line of work are you in?'

Dennis sat up straight and replied, 'I'm a copper. Dixon of Dock Green to you two.'

Sylvia smiled at him, raising her eyebrows, while Joyce brushed imaginary crumbs from her slacks. They all stared into their tea cups.

'Another slice, Dennis?' asked Sylvia, glancing at the clock.

'Best go,' sighed Dennis, 'On duty at 1 o' clock.'

After he left, Joyce cleared away the tea tray, clattering the cups unnecessarily. She had noticed how Dennis looked at Sylvia. Never occurred to the twit that she and Sylvia were not in need of company. Ironic that he thought that they were alone, and needed his presence. And a bit irritating how Sylvia pandered to him. Another slice, Dennis? I'll give him another slice! She resented how men gravitated to Sylvia. She was certainly a lovely woman, but she certainly wasn't available to him, or any other man.

Sylvia had enjoyed the visit. They had not really made friends with the new neighbours since they moved here, two months ago. Joyce had inherited the house from her uncle Eric. He had bought it with a win on the pools, a couple of years before he died. A heart attack at the Old Moseley Arms, when he was playing dominoes. At least he died happy, with his mates, Phil and Les. Never had any children himself, so his loss was their gain. Now Sylvia wanted to make new friends.

Dennis hurried along to work, with head bent. He really needed to summon his courage and speak to Sylvia. She would be just right for him. Life could be difficult, and he was 35 all ready. Would love to be able to settle down, but it seemed unlikely at the moment. The Policeman's ball was coming up in a couple of weeks, and he would look a right berk if he turned up alone. Again. He hadn't had much practice dancing, but he was sure he would pick it up.

Promptly at 5.30, Sylvia put the shepherd's pie on the table. The steam rose from the mashed potatoes, and the smell of mint from the garden filled the room. She looked at Joyce, who smiled at her, before digging in with the serving spoon, and ladling a heap on her plate. She handed her the gravy boat, with the willow pattern on it; a farewell gift from her old colleagues.

The red jelly pudding with tinned peaches was Joyce's favourite. She nodded enthusiastically when Sylvia brought it in. With just a dribble of Carnation milk. Together they ate, each glancing at their dishes, and then at each other. They washed it down with a cup of Brook Bond Dividend tea. Sylvia was saving the stamps to help out at Christmas.

Afterwards they followed their evening routine. Sylvia washed and Joyce dried.

'Popped into Curry's earlier today,' said Joyce, as she wiped the last saucepan and hung it on its hook. 'Asked them about hiring a television set. Have to work out if we can afford it. There's a licence fee of top ...'

Sylvia smiled, and squeezed her arm. Joyce refused to let her go out to work, and there was no point in bringing it up again. She was determined to support them with the money she earned at the dress factory. Sylvia kissed her softly on the cheek, and Joyce flushed.

'I'm going to see if I can get a bit of overtime,' said Joyce.

Then she built up the fire, adding just a few coals. Enough to last until bedtime. She lit a Park Drive, and inhaled. Perhaps she would have to give up smoking, if they hired a television. Or perhaps she could cut down. Imagine, having a telly! She knew that Sylvia would be proud. And, eventually, a hoover, maybe. Sylvia wasn't going to go without anything she would have had if she'd said 'yes' to Terry, just before they moved from Nottingham.

Sylvia gazed at the flames in the hearth. It was beautiful, making a home with Joyce. Her life had changed in ways she couldn't have imagined. Joyce made her feel safe. And wanted. She hadn't even realised before, that sex between two women was possible! But she loved it when Joyce suckled and entered her.

Next morning, the door knocker announced the arrival of Dennis. Joyce tightened her mouth and shook her head.

'Almost time for elevens,' he said, 'so I bought some Eccles cakes in the hopes of getting a cuppa with you.'

He picked up the bottle of milk from the door-step , hoisting it above his head like a white flag, as he stepped over the threshold.

The three sat down. Joyce and Sylvia in the arm chairs, and Dennis on the dining chair. Joyce glared at the clock, and then out of the window.

'To be honest,' began Dennis, 'there was something …'

Joyce leaned forward in her chair and put her cup down on the side table.

Sylvia sat back in her chair and pulled her skirt further down her legs.

'You know I'm a copper?' he said, 'Well, it's a bit awkward, you see …'

Joyce took a huge bite from her Eccles cake, and chewed it whilst holding eye contact with him, until he looked away.

'Every Christmas we have this policeman's ball at the Tally Ho …' he continued.

'Does the tax-payer fund it?' asked Joyce.

Sylvia frowned at her.

'Sounds lovely,' she said. 'Do you like dancing?'

'No,' he said. 'Absolutely hate it, but we're expected to go. They think you're a bit weird if you don't. And I, well I haven't got … I need … Perhaps … You see …'

Joyce and Sylvia stared at him. Neither moved. Dennis studied his hands which he was wringing. Then they all picked up their Eccles cakes, and finished them in silence.

'I wondered if you might understand,' he said, looking at Joyce.

'Understand what?' Joyce asked.

'Well, you know how it is…' he stuttered.

'How what is?' urged Sylvia.

'Haven't got a girlfriend.' he said, 'Never have had.'

'And how did you think that we could help?' asked Joyce, wiping her fingers on her slacks.

'Well,' he paused, then looking at Sylvia, said. 'I need a lady … to take to the dance…'

Sylvia had had many offers from men to take her to dances, take her to the cinema, or for an afternoon walk in the park. She had never heard such a miserable and awkward suggestion before. When Ronnie Hall had asked her out, he couldn't stop staring at her boobs. When Carl Morris had suggested the pictures, he hinted that they could have fun on the back row. Even the shy Kevin Walker had blushed and stammered when he spoke to her. But Sylvia noticed none of these things in Dennis.

The lack of them made her pause.

Joyce's eyes fired bullets across the room at him.

She knew men found Sylvia dainty and charming. Probably thought she would make a lovely wife. Except for one blindingly obvious thing. Like Joyce, Sylvia just wasn't attracted to men. But they seemed unaware. Thought they were two women living together through lack of opportunity. Had been left on the shelf. A pair of sad Old Maids. A gentle smile crossed her lips as she looked back at the unhappy Dennis.

Dennis, it turned out, was under no such illusions. Recognised the loving bond between them. Understood it. Had noticed Joyce stroke the back of Sylvia's hair when they turned away as he was leaving. Since falling in love with Andy, he sensed these things. Knew what being afraid of being caught out felt like. Had arrested queer men himself. Some had ended up in jail. Now he was terrified that his colleagues would guess his secret. So, he really needed a lady to take to the ball this year. And he hoped these two would help him out.

'I'm,' stuttered Dennis, 'You know… a friend of Dorothy.'

'I think I understand,' said Sylvia. 'A lady to take to the dance, but not to court afterwards?'

Dennis nodded several times, looking from one woman to the other, and back again.

Joyce widened her eyes. 'You're not going, are you, Sylvia?'

'Yes, my love,' said Sylvia. 'I want to help Dennis out. He's one of us.'

'What?' said Joyce, leaning forward in her chair. 'What do you mean? One of us, are you?'

She leapt to her feet, and stood next to the trembling Dennis.

'Bit queer, are you?'

Dennis nodded but didn't speak.

'Have you got … someone, you know … special?' Joyce asked.

'Oh aye, 'he replied. 'Andy. He's a copper as well. Been together a few years now but, you know …'

'And is he …?' asked Sylvia.

'Yes. He's going to the ball with the landlady from the Old Mo.,' said Dennis. 'She understands a lot, does Ivy.'

'Right,' said Joyce, turning to Sylvia. 'Better run you up a new dress at the weekend. Blue would look nice. Or pink?'

Sylvia poured them all another cuppa, from the big teapot.

Jenny and Diane — 1974

From the nurse's home windows of Nuffield House, she could see the smoke. Heard the explosion of a bomb. Boom! Right in the centre of Birmingham on a Friday night. Jenny had just finished putting her uniform on, ready to start the night shift. She sprinted across the road to the QE hospital. She was not alone. Streams of nurses were running towards the Casualty department, fastening the silver buckles on their belts as they ran. Adjusting their frilly caps.

Pausing at the entrance, they heard the second bomb in the distance. Boom! Boom!

Policemen started rushing out of the station opposite, on Livery Street. Wide-eyed and clutching their domed hats.

All nurses had been trained to respond to a major incident, but had never expected to do so. Each looked at the others. Matron was nowhere to be seen.

'Go to your usual wards,' shouted Jenny.

They followed her instruction. Not because she was the senior, but because no-one else could think straight. As they pounded up the stairs, stifled sobs could be heard. Someone screamed. Two nurses held hands.

Then a message was passed along, telling them all to go back to the hospital entrance, where Matron was now waiting. They tumbled and rushed down the stairs. Someone's shoe fell off, and was trampled. Matron's eyes were darting left and right. Gulping for breath, she confirmed that there had been two bomb blasts in the city centre. Numerous casualties were on their way to the hospital. Most were in a serious condition. Many had been killed.

The nurses rushed around. The air was heavy. Blood-soaked casualties were wheeled in hurriedly. Patients were treated and sent to wards.

Or to the mortuary.

Sodden dressings overflowed from the bins. The metallic stench of blood. Porters were sent to replenish supplies. Even old Joe, due for retirement at the end of the month, started to run.

Hours passed. No banter. No jokes. No going for coffee breaks.

Usually, at 7.30am, the day staff would take over. But most had all ready been there all night. They struggled on. 182 patients needed care. Doctors shouted orders. Nurses snapped that they were already doing all they could. Some felt guilty for going to the toilet, where they took the opportunity to have a good sob. Or a fag. Wondering if anyone they knew and loved had been injured.

Jenny worried about her uncle Dennis who was a police sergeant. He would be in the thick of it. Then thought of Diane, who would be meeting her for breakfast, as usual, after the night shift ended. She had no way of forewarning her that she couldn't leave the hospital on time. She knew that Diane was not always sympathetic if things didn't go her way. Perhaps, with the bombs going off …

By early afternoon, some were told to go back to the nurse's home for a rest and a sleep.

Come back as soon as possible.

Jenny arrived back at her room, carrying crisps.

In front of the window, with smoke still visible in the distance, stood Dianne.

'What bloody time do you call this? Two o'clock? I've been here since Eight o'clock. Where the hell …?' shouted Diane.

Jenny undid the blue packet with the salt, and shook it over the crisps. She peered at the wine stain on her floor, from an impromptu party. Only last week …

'What's going on?' snapped Diane. 'You were …'

'Did you hear about the bombs?' asked Jenny.

Diane had heard the bombs and seen the news on television. She had sat with tears running down her face. A rotten end to a bloody awful day. Life wasn't easy, being a woman who owned a building business. She'd spent the previous day finishing the construction of a porch. She looked at her work with satisfaction. For the last few days everything had gone well. The customer, Glenys Johnson, was delighted with the job, and gave Diane a hug. Tea and biscuits were shared.

That final Friday afternoon, when presenting the bill, she met the husband for the first time.

'You said a builder,' he shouted at his wife. 'Not a bloody woman.'

'Shush, Brian,' said Glenys.

He stormed around the porch, looking for faults in the building. Finding none he turned around to Diane, red-faced and sweating.

'You a bleeding lezzie, or what?' he asked. 'What the hell you think you're doing, building a porch?'

He lifted the bill in front of her face and tore it up.

'Don't think I didn't see the way you looked at my missus earlier.' He ranted. 'Would never have left her alone in the house with you if I'd known.' Storming back into the house he slammed the door.

'Sorry Bab; I'll make sure you get your money,' said Glenys, hurrying after Diane as she left. Catching her arm she said, 'Meet me in the Old Mo later, love. I'll give you a cheque.'

Diane had nothing planned for that evening. Jenny was on nights this week. Thankfully this was her last shift. They would meet for breakfast next morning, as always, in her room. Hot buttered toast. Making love before Jenny snuggled down to sleep. Happy Saturdays. It amused Diane that men weren't allowed in the nurse's home.

But she was.

The talk in the Old Mo on that Friday night had been about moving some bloke's body across Brum via the airport to Dublin. IRA apparently. Blew himself up trying to plant a bomb in Coventry. For some reason over a thousand cops had escorted his coffin. Diane wasn't interested. She watched the door waiting for Glenys. She really needed this damned cheque. Had worked bloody hard for it. What a tosser her old man had turned out to be. Why would a lovely woman like her …?

Then Glenys walked in. Diane had never noticed

before what a sultry smile she had. What a neat body. Looked good in jeans and a tight tee shirt. She beckoned her across to her table.

'Let me get you another drink,' said Glenys and sailed across to the bar, leaving a waft of Lily of the Valley behind her. 'Hubby's out tonight…'

They heard the first bomb in the distance. Boom! Locked eyes, with hands over their mouths. Then the second. Boom! Boom!

The framed picture of the Queen shuddered. At first the pub was silent as everyone held their breath. Then the hushed questions. Then the shouting. Drinks were flowing. People bustled to the door to look out towards the city. Smoke billowing. Some hastened home to their families. Others formed huddles and carried on the supping and chatting.

Then the old codgers went back to playing darts.

Diane went home and slept fitfully. By 8am she was at the nurse's home, waiting in Jenny's room for her to come off her shift. In her hand was a scribbled note that had been pushed under her door earlier that morning. How had Glenys found her address? Of course; it was on the invoice. She put the kettle on and waited. Made herself some toast. Where on earth was Jenny? Her shift had finished at 8am.

The note was succinct.

Same time. Same place. Tonight? G.

She screwed it up and shoved it in her jeans pocket.

When Jenny finally arrived, Diane was scowling. Partners were supposed to support each other. But where had Jenny been when Diane needed to tell her about her rotten day? Instead of being remorseful, Jenny had just asked her about the bombs. Then sat staring at the floor.

'I need to get some sleep Di. Back on duty at 6 o'clock.'

'It's your weekend off,' yelled Diane. 'What about us?'

Jenny lifted her face at last and looked at Diane. But all she could see were images of injured patients. Some had been impaled by wooden furniture. Many had their clothes burnt on to their bodies. A coppery smell, like a barbeque. Screaming and sobbing. Or, worse, silence. So many of them. So many. She got into bed wordlessly, without undressing, and fell asleep quickly. Still holding the crisp packet.

Diane crept out of the room. She hadn't realised that dating a nurse would be so frustrating. Shifts being changed at the last minute. Weekend leave cancelled. Now this. She couldn't believe that Jenny was actually going to go back to work on her day off. Should have refused. This was their time. All this 'Angels in Cloaks' rubbish. What about her? *Charity begins at home.* She'd slogged her guts out all week. Been looking forward to going out for a drink and a dance tonight. But, just like that, Jenny had rolled over and agreed to go back to work.

At a loose end, Diane decided to go to the city centre market. The Bull Ring usually had loads of interesting stalls. She'd pick up some cheap stuff. As she approached Digbeth, she found it cordoned off within a mile radius. Smoke still rising. Pungent air. Rescue people still searching. Ambulances. Panda cars. People standing around the edge of the cordon. Some crying, others calling out to the rescue workers.

'Have you seen …?'

'Bloody hell. Everything's going wrong for me today,' she thought.

She got the 50 bus back to Kings Heath Street market. Only four miles from the bombing, but life goes on. Perhaps buy a couple of records. Music blared from Douggie's Vinyl Stall. He was singing along, waving his arms and smiling at the gathering crowd, who joined in the chorus.

'What's too painful to remember, we simply choose to forget…'

How bloody miserable. She wouldn't buy that one for sure. She and Jenny were in love. They'd been together nearly four months now and everything was going great. Sod off, Barbara Streisand. You don't do anything for me.

Diane watched as women moved forward to buy the records. Sad lot, really. Then Barry White came on. This was more like it.

'My kind of wonderful, that's what you are.'

She handed over the 45p, pressed the record to her chest and beamed. She'd play it at Jenny's tomorrow. Probably sing along to it. Let Jenny know how much she meant to her.

Diane wandered around. Clothes stalls with peasant blouses, bell bottom trousers and miniskirts. Nothing she fancied. Feeling peckish she mused, Poplar café or Ted's 'Ot Dogs stand on the corner?

The long hot sausage was slimy and steaming. Impaled into the white bread roll. Blood-red splashes of sauce and fiery mustard. She chewed whilst thinking of Jenny. Working on her time off. That woman needed a good talking to about standing up for herself.

Pottering around Woolworths, she spotted Glenys with her husband. They were buying loose biscuits. Brian was laughing. Glenys pressed his arm. Diane grinned to herself remembering all the ginger-nuts she had tucked into over the last couple of weeks, at their house. As Glenys turned aside, Brian slapped her on the bum. He was rewarded with a chuckle.

Diane fondled the crumpled note in her pocket, and cocked her head to one side. When Glenys caught sight of her, Diane raised her eyebrows and was acknowledged with a smile and an air kiss.

Tindall Street was welcoming in the moonlight. Diane could see the lights in the Old Moseley Arms window as she approached. Striding past the school opposite she glanced over and saw a figure rushing towards her. Waving a hammer, above his head. He smashed it into her skull.

Like cracking an egg. Crashing onto the pavement. Excruciating pain.

Diane glimpsed Brian's contorted face. Behind him, was Glenys, cackling with laughter.

She could hear the distant police sirens; too far away. *I need you here, she thought.* Before passing out.

On her break from duty in Casualty, Jenny sipped her coffee. She rehearsed in her mind how she would tell Diane that she would have to work Sunday night as well. Her throat tightened and she felt a knot in her stomach. It felt impossible to eat the egg mayo sandwich.

This is very hard to swallow.

Jenny saw the trolley being rushed through the entrance by two sweating ambulance men. Leaving her food, she brushed down her uniform dress. She fastened her buckled belt and straightened her frilly cap. Put on her professional face.

Approaching the new arrival, she did not recognise the blood-soaked face.

'Unconscious patient, love. Horrible head injury. Found on the path outside a pub,' the ambulance driver intoned.

Jenny sighed. They were still clearing up after the horrors of last night. Some of the survivors still hadn't been transferred to wards. Glancing around the department, she looked for an empty cubicle, then back at the ambulance men. She momentarily closed her eyes, then inhaled deeply.

'Another drunk?' she asked.

Penny and Hazel — 1978

The rain pelted down as she stumbled along the drive. Stared at the garden, overgrown since her dad died. Weeds starting to choke the struggling flowers. By the time her mother opened the door, she was drenched and shivering. Her long red hair fell helplessly in rat's tails. She looked down at her squelching sandals which she prepared to remove.

Pauline, her mum, did not make the best of herself. A shampoo and set every six weeks, and a bubble bath on Saturday nights. Punishingly thin. Her mouth turned down at the edges. Gave the impression that she spent hours trudging up and down streets in bad weather.

Penny hung up her soggy anorak. Sighed. Wandered into the sitting room. The gas fire was turned on, although it was early July. Damask grey wallpaper hung sedately. Crocheted cushions were plumped up. The hand-pegged hearth rug was brushed. A cloying whiff of spring flowers air freshener.

Pauline, as always, sat in her armchair and poured the tea. Penny reached over and accepted the cup. Royal Albert China. It always came out on Sunday afternoons, now. Ever since her husband died, Pauline treated her daughter's weekly visit as an occasion. She glanced at Penny's denim jeans, and checked shirt. Then brushed imaginary crumbs from her own crimplene skirt.

The clock on the mantlepiece marked time. Tick tock. Tick tock.

From what Penny heard at the Gay Centre, many women endured a rough time, coming out to their parents. Some lesbians were informed it was just a phase they were going through. Others refused to discuss it. One mother queried if this meant she also took drugs. Two religious women were excommunicated from their church. Occasionally parents took it on the chin, and wished their offspring well.

Penny's partner, Hazel, fared a bit better, yesterday. Previously her mum warned her not to tell her dad. Convinced he would have a nervous breakdown. But he simply said, 'Thank God. It means you won't get pregnant like your sister.' Then her mother, over custard creams, informed her Richard Lyons's wife left him. This meant he was 'back on the market again', if Hazel was interested.

Penny felt a sense of urgency to come out to Pauline. Her group of friends were planning their first trip to Gay Pride next weekend. They were angry about the unfair way lesbians and gays were treated. Always needing to hide. To pretend … Only last week, WH Smith banned Gay Times from their stores. Time to take action. Together the group would stand up and be counted. Go to their first Pride march, in London.

Away from her mates, Penny didn't feel brave. She knew of two women who were forced to have ECT when their sexuality was revealed. Sectioned under the mental health act, with the support of their parents. She rubbed her sweaty hands on her trousers.

And, of course, now that dad was gone …

Last night, she and her mates spent the evening creating banners and placards. 'Lesbians are everywhere.' 'Out and Proud.' Feeling confident. They looked at a copy of last year's Daily Mail. Its front-page photographic coverage of Pride. Lots of gays striding confidently along. Waving to the spectators and detractors. Singing gay anthems. Penny felt alarmed as she gripped the newspaper. Supposing that she was in the headlines this year? Nobody wanted their parents to find out by seeing their photo in the paper. Sweated at the thought. Penny was now the only one in their group who wasn't already out. Afraid of how her mum would react. She was urged to get it over with.

The gas fire popped and Pauline turned it down a little.

'I know he's been gone six months ... but I don't know which way to turn...' began Pauline.

Penny sighed. Her parents were married for nearly 25 years. Celebrated every anniversary with a meal at Poplar Road café. And yet ... Dutiful. The word sprang to mind whenever she considered their long marriage. Dutiful. And dull.

Penny's childhood had been a quiet one. An only child, with two polite parents.

'More potatoes, John?' Pauline would ask.

'No, thank you, dear,' he would reply, mopping his mouth with a gingham napkin.

'Anyway, I've taken his stuff to the Oxfam shop...' whispered Pauline.

When Penny met Hazel, it was an epiphany. Laughter. Shrieking. Lust and ...happiness. All this was new. Finding herself grinning at nothing, while at work. Suddenly nothing was too much trouble for her. Counting the hours 'til they would meet again. Re-playing the funny things Hazel had said ... They decided to rent a house together, in Grange Road. Sharing meals, rampant sex and the washing up.

Pauline carried through the rose-patterned plates holding the cheese on toast. One slice each, sparsely covered. Penny watched the melted cheese dripping over the edge of the toast. This was the best time to tell her about Hazel. While they were eating. Give her Mum chance to swallow it, while she was chewing a crust. *Tell her now. No, later. No, now …*

'Mum. How did you and dad know you loved each other?' she began.

Pauline's eyes widened, and she choked slightly. She stared out of the window, and seemed suddenly interested in the cat in next door's garden.

'How did …?' repeated Penny.

Picking up her embroidered napkin, Pauline dabbed her lips. Things were different back then. It wasn't about if you would marry, but who you would marry. She'd met John on her seventeenth birthday, at the local dance hall. Strange how it turned out. Every Saturday she and her friends went dancing together. Fun-filled nights. But one by one they all got boy-friends. Heavy hints were dropped that she needed to find a fella of her own, so she'd still fit in with the group.

When John asked her to dance, she was happy

to become one of the crowd. They started courting. Six months later, there was their first fumbling sexual encounter. Neither felt the need to repeat it any time soon.

'Got pregnant with you, straight away,' said Pauline, staring into the fire. She seemed to be having trouble swallowing her toast. 'Couldn't ask for an abortion as Uncle Frank was our family doctor. Forced to get married. Shotgun wedding.'

Penny sat bolt upright in her chair. This was the most intimate conversation they ever shared. Woman to woman. She turned off the fire, and removed her tank top. Pauline picked at the congealing food on her plate. Silence, and then …

'We just got on with it,' continued Pauline. 'Never wanted to get married or have kids. But I was in the club, so …'

What a waste of a life! Why on earth hadn't her mum left dad years ago? And now he died so young … Everyone talked about him as though he was a perfect husband. Not that he was a nasty bloke. Just cold. Distant. Boring.

'Did you? … Did you ever love dad?' stuttered Penny.

Pauline fixed her gaze on her rapidly chilling tea, and added another spoon of sugar.

'I've no idea what you mean by love. What I know is that there was a clean, ironed shirt every day for work. His tea was on the table at 6 o'clock every night. I kept a tidy house and was careful with his money. And we stayed together 'til he died.'

Penny stared at the window, where the rose bush was beating against the glass. Loose petals stuck to the glass. Noticed the wind blowing the trees, as the sky darkened. She now realised why she was an only child.

'Mum, can I tell you something?' began Penny. 'You know Hazel, who I share a house with? Well…'

Pauline glared. Slammed down her fork. Her face was a starched white sheet. 'Don't say anything that can't be unsaid,' she snapped. 'I've made some jam tarts for pudding.'

Penny followed her into the kitchen, where Pauline was wrenching the lid off the biscuit tin.

'Don't!' she wept. 'Don't say it. Don't be so bloody selfish.'

Penny sank onto the three-legged kitchen stool, which felt fragile under her weight.

'I saw you with her. Kissing her in front of your lounge window,' shouted Pauline, crashing the lid onto the draining board. 'When I called round your house to ask you to come straight to the hospital …

I had to walk round the block for a while, til it was safe for me to come in.'

The two women locked eyes.

'Shameless …' sobbed Pauline.

Silence. The sweet treats were untouched.

'Do you think I was never tempted?' cried Pauline. 'Your uncle Dennis … But I had more decency …'

She rammed a jam tart into her mouth.

Penny clasped her hands together. She needed to do this. Get on with it. Stop acting like a child. *Do it, Penny.*

'We … a group of us … next Saturday. Going on the Gay Pride march. In London,' whispered Penny.

'Over my dead body,' screamed Pauline. 'What the hell do you think that would do to your grandma?'

Later, as Penny cried in Hazel's arms, she mulled things over. At school, the other girls had taped photos of Elvis Presley or Billy Fury under their desk lids. She hadn't made a conscious decision to stick pictures of Dusty Springfield and Sandy Shaw under her own. They had all just done as they pleased. It went on from there.

'You've got to live your own life,' murmured Hazel. 'She made her choices …'

The night before Pride they all gathered at the Gay Centre in town. A motley group of different ages. Most dressed in jeans and shirts. Or blouses. Short hair. Some in Doc Martin's. Wearing labyris symbols around their necks, or pink triangle badges. Putting finishing touches to their flags. Excited. Painting and pasting. Cans of beer, Crisps. Chocolate. Reminding each other why they were going…

Then all started singing;

Sing if you're glad to be gay
Sing if you're happy that way

Most only knew the chorus, but it was enough. So, they repeated it. Again, and again. They were sisters. Standing together. They covered each other's backs. Looking round the room Penny felt powerful and supported. This was her life. Out and Proud.

Later, in bed, relaxed and intimate, Hazel reminded Penny of the rest of the words of the song. About police harassment, and discrimination against gays. She was glad they were finally doing something about it. Not hiding. Raising the roof. Walking tall. Standing up against the establishment. The Pride march was the first step forward. And, afterwards …

Penny felt a knot of fear. She didn't want to be pressured. Wasn't at all sure she wanted to come out publicly yet. Didn't want to cause extra sadness to her grieving mum. No idea what her dad would have said if he was still here. Mum was right. What about Gran? Beautiful Gran, who loved her and stuck up for her always. But Gran wouldn't understand dykes. Would be mortified by a photo of her grand-daughter in the paper. On a Gay Pride march.

Penny didn't go to sleep. She spent the night summoning the courage to tell Hazel she couldn't go. There were other ways to be strong in the lesbian community. She thought about setting up a telephone help-line. Lesbian line. Supporting women who were struggling with their sexuality. That's something she could do. Without upsetting her family.

At 6.30a.m. she shook Hazel awake and told her she wasn't going. Couldn't bear to hurt her mum and her Gran. Especially now that dad ... Wasn't worth the upset ... Who knows? Next time?

'You must be bloody joking!' Hazel had shouted, thumping the pillow.

Doors slammed. A mug of coffee was thrown at the wall. It splintered and dripped down onto the banner. Smudged the word 'Proud'. Penny, crying, started to dab it dry. Hazel snatched it away.

'Proud?' asked Hazel. 'You're pathetic! Pitiful, Penny'.

They were both sobbing when Jackie and Helen rang the doorbell at 7. 30. Wearing berets with rainbows pinned to them. Clutching their banners and laughing. They shouted to them to hurry up and get to the bus stop. The London train wouldn't wait for them if they were late.

At first, they were puzzled by Penny. Disbelief! Disappointment. Derision. The three 'sisters' glared at her. Helen looked at her watch and tapped its face.

'OK, I know it's hard, Penny,' said Jackie, softening. 'It nearly killed me to tell my mum. Perhaps some other time?'

'Next year,' promised Penny, watching as Hazel rushed off towards the bus stop without saying goodbye. Jackie and Helen waved to her as they ran. They were no longer smiling.

Penny curled up on the sofa with a cup of coffee. What was going on? She'd felt oppressed by Hazel today. Yet her pals were all going off to London to march against oppression. Her Mum had made it clear that she disapproved of her. It would wreck the family if she went on the march. But, wasn't motherly love supposed to be unconditional? Her head was throbbing.

There was a hammering on the door. An insistent banging. Pauline stood on the doorstep shaking.

'I need to talk, 'she started.

Penny waved her into the sitting room, where she perched on the arm of the Ikea chair.

'I've had a think…' Pauline said, wringing her hands.

Penny looked at her stone-faced.

'About what I said …'

Penny leaned back and folded her arms. She tilted her head on one side.

'In my day …' continued Pauline, 'It just wasn't done …'

'No …,' said Penny.

'I'd made my bed and …,' said Pauline

The two women sat in silence, both staring at the stained red carpet.

Then Pauline described her wretched days since Penny had called round. She didn't want Penny to waste her life. Her own marriage hadn't been miserable. Just …pointless. Recently she struggled through sleepless nights. Still wished Penny could settle down with a nice bloke. But … she knew now it wouldn't happen. Seemed very queer to her, for a woman to want another woman. But what did she know about anything?

'Go to your Pride thing with those friends,' she said. 'Let me pay for a taxi so you can catch up with them at the station.'

As Penny climbed into the taxi, Pauline leaned in and gave her a hug.

'Your Gran doesn't read the Sunday papers ...'

Penny nodded, blinking.

'I want you to be, well, ... loved ...' stammered Pauline.

The taxi pulled away. Finally, the sun broke through the clouds.

Glancing out of the back window, she saw Pauline, trudging home.

Katy and Bronwen — 1988

They met in a front room in Springfield Road. Eight of them this time. Sitting in arm chairs, on stools or beanbags. Dressed in jeans and shirts. Incense sticks burning. Wind chimes in the corner. Book shelves revealing titles from Toni Morrisson, Doris Lessing, George Elliot, Maya Angelou … *You get the picture?*

The women's consciousness-raising group was advertised in 'Spare Rib.' About challenging the patriarchy. Refusing to take on traditional roles. Clause 28 was the agenda topic that evening. The government's homophobic attempt to stop homosexuality being promoted in schools. Intended to protect children from evil gays! It was Katy's fifth meeting, and she was elected to lead. Discussion started with some people's belief that gay people were paedophiles. Caroline worked in child protection. Said that all the paedophiles she had met were straight men. There was spirited discussion as they drained their glasses and ate the crisps and peanuts.

Katy asked the group to consider the idea of lesbians having babies of their own. Or adopting. Cutting out the middle man. Should it be allowed? Would the government act against that next? Why should they be refused the opportunity of motherhood, just because they didn't want sex with men?

Voices were raised. Some women felt angry at the idea. It was just aping heterosexuals. Once you were dragged down with a baby it was too late to change your mind. Taking your freedom … Feeding into the patriarchy by producing the next generation of workers. As for clause 28. Bloody Thatcher!

'I'd love a baby, actually,' stammered Katy.

'I understand,' whispered Caroline, in reply. The only group member to agree.

Back at home, Katy shared the night's events with Bronwen. Mentioned that she sometimes wondered if she would like to be a mother. Now that she was 30.

'You knew when we got together, we couldn't …' laughed Bronwen. 'I haven't got the right equipment.'

Katy nodded.

'Let's book a holiday instead,' suggested Bronwen.

'Consolation prize?' asked Katy.

They uncorked a bottle of wine and each sat with their own thoughts. Strange how things changed in the last few weeks. Since they went on the Lesbian Strength march in London. The first time they met a lesbian with a baby. A baby she gave birth to herself. No man involved! Neither felt able to ask how it happened. On the coach on the way back Bronwen told Katy she sympathised with the woman. Knew she would regret becoming a mother. Being tied down with a sprog for the rest of your life. No money. Bread-snappers. No free time. Holidays spent building sand castles. Dull as ditchwater.

Katy agreed. The death knell to promotion at work either, as child care took priority. Sleepless nights. Silent sex so as not to disturb them. Screaming brats. Cuddling together on the back seat of the coach both smug as they reflected on their lives. Being together for eight years was a miracle for them both. Each usually got bored with girlfriends after about six months. But this time they just knew. Settled down. Rented a terraced house on Avenue Road. Just opposite the park. Theatre trips, curry nights, holidays abroad, gym memberships.

Being a qualified veterinary nurse, Katy found work in the local animal sanctuary. She loved her job. Got along well with her colleagues. Enjoyed helping the animals to settle into their new surroundings. Taught the dogs to be house-trained. Ensured they were given treatments they needed. Delighted each day by the welcome she got from them all. Dogs wagging tails and jumping up. Cats circling her legs and purring. Even the chickens and pigs ran to greet her. The best bit was when they were re-homed. She always waved them off tearfully. Glad that they would now have the life they deserved.

Bronwen was a solicitor. Bored with her job, but at least it paid the bills. They were saving up to buy a house together. At least, she was saving up. Katy earned so little that after she had paid her share of the bills, she didn't have much left. When younger, Bronwen wanted to be a film-maker. Would love to make documentaries. Or dramas. Her dad wouldn't hear of it. Pressured her into studying law. Now she spent her days with couples who were divorcing. Listening to all their grievances. Felt glad that lesbians couldn't get married. Was just the sort of thing that Katy would be into. Smiled as she thought of her sentimentality.

On the Saturday night they went to watch a film about trekking in Nepal. Both were fascinated. Images of maroon-dressed nuns walking across snowy hill-tops. Intricately painted mandalas. Nepalis walking at daybreak swirling their prayer wheels. Stupas on every path. It was all so unlike their own lives. Later they considered what such a trip would be like. Bronwen wanted to find out.

Wednesday night was Bronwen's time with her pool team. They played in the back room at the Malt Shovel on Brighton Road. Really handy as she could get the 50-bus straight home. A couple of pints of Guiness, a few laughs with her mates. A great night. None of them showed any interest in Nepal. They did mention clause 28. There was to be a protest march and they would all go. To lighten the mood, Bronwen mentioned Katy's daft suggestion about having a baby. Set them all off laughing again. So funny!

That night, candles lit, they had sex on the rug in front of the fire. Gave each other pleasure. Holding tight. Stroking. Loving. Then lay smiling at each other before stumbling up to bed. Cuddled up beneath their gingham quilt. Feeling safe. Wanted.

Women's Adventure Trekking sent their brochure. There were options of doing twelve days or three weeks trekking. Various grades of strenuousness. It all looked wonderful. The stuff of dreams. Bronwen studied it until the pages were creased and folded. She suggested to Katy that they start with one of the easiest treks. Perhaps Pokhara? They could do more arduous treks next year when they were fitter. In her lunch break she had rung the owner of the company to get more information. It was exciting. Different. The Helambu trek sounded great. It was led by a woman who had been a nun. Inspirational! There was so much more out there in the world to discover. They could visit the Swayambhunath temple in Kathmandu before setting off on the trail. Have a trip out to the mediaeval village of Bhaktapur after their return.

'Who knows?' Bronwen asked Katy. 'Nepal this year. Africa next!'

Katy was at work the next day. Administering medications to the dogs. Gazing into their trusting eyes. Fighting back a tear when they offered her a paw. Trimming the nails of the cats while they tried to bat her. Grooming the horses; those beautiful giants. She was surprised to see Caroline walking across the field to join her. Didn't realise she knew where she worked. They sat together in the corner of the field, admiring the animals.

'What brings you here?'

Turned out that Caroline and her partner, Josie, wanted to have a baby. Katy was the only woman she thought would understand. Had no idea how to go about it. She had heard that there was a service where you could get artificial insemination. Had to pay for it. Did Katy know anything about it? Katy had no idea, but was intrigued.

Katy and Bronwen went out for a curry on Saturday night. Shabab's balti on the Ladypool road was their favourite. The smell of garlic and spices met them from the door. Stepping into the dimly lit café felt exotic. Henna patterned wallpaper graced the walls. Glass topped tables and metal chairs. Balti dishes made of steel. Hindustani background music. They both chose the delicious mixed vegetable and lentil balti. Served with naan breads. And cool, fresh raita. It felt like an authentic Indian experience. One of their Asian friends told them that only white people drank lassi. They enjoyed it anyway. Rumour had it that the balti dish had been invented locally, in Birmingham, to Anglicise the dish. The waiter, when questioned, would rock his head slowly from side to side and reply 'Maybe. Maybe not.'

'We'll be eating like this every day in Nepal,' laughed Bronwen.

'Sure will, 'replied Katy, grinning, 'Or something like it …'

Their Sunday Walk took them over the Malvern Hills. Good practice for their forthcoming trek. Bronwen wondered if they should get a Nepali phrase book. And they would need better walking boots. What about vaccinations? Water sterilising tablets. They marched over to British camp. Bronwen taking the lead. Katy struggling to keep up.

They were both glad to flop down in Saint Anne's Well café for lunch, at the end. The old café, Victorian in design. One of their stomping grounds for years. Munching the home-made veggie burgers. Drinking water straight from the spring next to the door. Bronwen described their plans in detail to John, the pony-tailed owner. Waving her arms and laughing, she explained her ideas to the rest of the diners.

'So, will we be walking for 17 days non-stop, in Nepal?' asked Katy.

Bronwen shoved her cupcake into her mouth. Wiped the cream off her chin. Then suggested that they needed to develop a training plan. Over the months they needed to be fitter, and able to do the trek.

A few weeks later, Caroline and Josie invited them round for supper. They walked the short distance to their home in Highbury Road, clutching two bottles of wine. It was always good to meet new people, and Bronwen was excited. Neither of them was in her pool team, or the football club.

Josie loved cooking. Smells of fresh herbs met them as they went into the sitting room. Fascinating to see inside other people's homes. Katy loved the Laura Ashley wall paper and the crocheted cushions. Around the room were reminders of past holidays. A painted wooden bowl from the Gambia. A copper singing bowl from Nepal. Framed pictures of masked parades in Vienna. A small statue of Shiva from India. A brass plaque of Tara, goddess of wisdom in Tibet.

'It's so homely here,' said Katy.

Caroline and Josie smiled. They had lived here for six years. Bought the house when they were both 24. Quite young to make such a big step, but they had no doubts. Love at first sight when they met in the Fox.

'All these places you've travelled, 'said Bronwen. 'I'm so envious. Me and katy are going trekking in Nepal soon. Can't wait ...'

They carried their wine into the dining room. The table was covered with a lace tablecloth from Venice. There was a vegetable lasagne. Cheese bubbling on the top. A green salad with olive-wood servers, bought in Palestine. Crispy garlic bread with butter seeping through the edges. Served on green-rimmed plates.

'Our travelling days are over, 'said Caroline. 'We've going to start a family.'

Bronwen and Katy both paused with the forks half way to their mouths.

'What?' asked Bronwen.

Josie and Caroline had arranged an appointment with BPAS. Apparently, you could get inseminated there. The company checked out the donors for AIDs and genetic stuff. Caroline was keen to go ahead. At 30, she felt the clock was ticking. Josie looked forward to teaching the kid to swim. And ride a bike. They'd even got as far as asking Caroline's mum to child-mind three days a week, so that Caroline could work part-time. Her parents hadn't been as keen as they hoped.

'Sounds wonderful, 'said Katy, beaming at them.

'Absolutely great,' added Bronwen, spooning more lasagne into her mouth.

Bronwen and Katy started planning for future treks. Increased their physical activities. Swimming before work. Hill-walking on Sunday. Bronwen even signed up at the climbing wall. Still undecided which trek to go for. Each one was enticing. Getting ready for their big event.

Katy arrived home from work one day to see Bronwen smiling and excited.

'I've found the perfect trek,' she yelled. 'We could go in October for three weeks. Or next April …'

'Gosh, 'said Katy. 'How much …?'

They needed to book leave from work. Katy wrung her hands. She had never left the animals for three weeks before. Always just took a week away at a time. Missed them so much. And Bronwen would need to find a decent solicitor to cover her cases while she was away. Not easy.

'And, when we come back …?' asked Katy.

'What?' replied Bronwen. 'The world will be our oyster'

Katy listened as Bronwen explained. One of her dreams was to take a gap year and travel. Hadn't been able to afford it when she was younger but now … Could use the cash she'd been saving to buy a house. Once in a lifetime chance … Wanted to explore Africa. Safari in Kenya. Table top mountains. Sail in a dugout canoe in the Gambia. Perhaps climb Kilimanjaro in Tanzania. Then, maybe move on to India …Mumbai, Kerala and Goa…

'The years are passing by,' said Bronwen. 'Do it while we're still youngish …'

Katy examined her finger nails. Trekking had never

appealed to her. She enjoyed their short breaks in Spain and Corfu. Beaches. Palm trees. She saw that Bronwen was happy. Making plans had invigorated her. A gap year from the job she hated would be good for her.

Did Katy need to go along with her?

Tuesday night was Sheila's Bar. In the back room at The Station on the High Street. Each week a notice was pinned to the door stating 'Ladies only.' The women inside did not seem ladylike. Short hair and Doc Martens. Drinking pints and being boisterous. Some smooching opening. Others pointedly ignoring their ex-girlfriends.

'Just orange juice for me for me, I'm afraid,' laughed Caroline.

'You bugger,' smiled Josie. 'You said I could tell them.'

They had done it! Caroline had become pregnant at first try. Inseminated while lying in Josie's arms. Smug smiles. Josie put her arm around Caroline's shoulder and pulled her close. Kissed her cheek. They wanted to talk about little else. Baby clothes. Cots. What names should they choose? Perhaps Sarah for a girl? Or Claire? And Adam for a boy? Or James?

'Shall I crochet a baby shawl?' offered Katy. 'Or bootees?'

Bronwen stifled a yawn.

'You two can have first refusal at babysitting if you like …' grinned Josie.

'No, thanks pal,' said Bronwen, smiling. 'We're hoping to take a gap year. Do some travelling. Get about a bit.'

Caroline looked at Katy. 'Putting the baby thing on hold until you come back? 'She asked.

'Or forever!' replied Bronwen. 'Not really our thing.'

Katy smiled and stared at the floor.

One night when Bronwen came back from work exhausted. Needed a long break. Wanted to start their gap year in spring. Instead of trekking in Nepal. Just go for it …Could start in Morocco … then …

'Don't think I could leave the animals at the sanctuary …' mumbled Katie. 'Not for a whole year.'

She would be willing to just do a two-week trek in November. What about Italy? The Alps looked beautiful. Back in time for Christmas. Doing all the Christmassy things with their friends. But a whole year? The whole idea was a bit rushed. Just because Bronwen didn't like her job …

'What?' shouted Bronwen. 'Shall I go on my own?'

There were many things Katy didn't want to leave behind for a year. Not just the animals. She wanted to see her mum at Christmas and on Mother's Day. Her friends at the consciousness-raising group. The rounders team. Just going out for Friday night drinks at the Fox. Hopefully babysitting for Caroline some-times. Too much to leave behind just to look at other countries.

'We could watch travel videos,' she said. 'Have the best of both worlds.'

'So, you'd be happy for me to go travelling for a year without you?' snapped Bronwen. 'Wouldn't you miss me at all? I thought …'

'You don't have to go,' answered Katy.

Weeks passed. Caroline and Josie amassed baby things. Bronwen amassed travel guides. Katy worked extra unpaid hours at the sanctuary. In fact, Katy was absent from home quite a lot. Bronwen refused to show interest in all the extra letters she got. Her many phone calls. Refused to ask where she was going when she left the house in smart new clothes, and was gone all

Caroline and Josie announced the birth of their little girl, Rachel. Weighing in at seven pounds and screaming herself hoarse every time Katy and Bron-wen visited. Caroline described how she was now able to distinguish the different cries and what they meant. Josie was convinced that Rachel was starting to smile. They rambled on about breast feeding and vaccinations …

The five of them shared a summer picnic in Kings Heath Park. Not easy to talk when Rachel was squawking. Teething apparently. Could go on for months. Josie and Caroline were exhausted. Sleep deprived. In fact, they were taking it in turns to sleep in the spare room so that at least one of them could get some rest. They were surprised when Bronwen told them she would be travelling for a year alone.

Bronwen would be setting off on her gap year travels next September. It had taken a while to get her boss to agree to the time off, but now she could plan ahead. She tried to enthuse her friends about her plans. A whole year of discovery. Mountains, seas, deserts… So much to see … and do …

'What will you be doing to fill your time while she's gone, Katy?' asked Caroline.

'Well,' replied Katy, 'I haven't had chance to tell Bronwen this yet. 'Kept it to myself in case it didn't work out.'

'What?' asked Bronwen holding eye contact.

'I've just had it confirmed …' Katy continued.

'What?' shouted Bronwen.

'I've been accepted at Cambridge university,' she said. 'Going to study to become a veterinary surgeon. Yes; I'll be a proper vet! ...' She screwed her eyes up and shook her head, laughing.

Late September saw the four friends gathered at New Street train station. Josie was holding a squirming Rachel, who was repeatedly passed between her and Caroline. Bronwen carried a backpack and a holdall. Checking her passport and tickets. She was catching the train to London before heading to Heathrow. Katy was carrying her text books and stationery in a briefcase and a toolbox of surgical instruments. She was catching the train to Cambridge, to start her studies.

Bronwen and Katy kissed each other. Would things be the same when they returned?

'Will you still love me when I come back tanned and penniless?' Bronwen asked.

'Will you still love me when I'm permanently stinking of pig shit?' Katy laughed.

One final hug and they went their separate ways.

Caroline and Josie watched them part. Josie pulled Rachel close and kissed her soft hot cheek. She had finally drifted off to sleep.

Pippa and Kim — 1992

There was no point peering along Vicarage Road from their sixth-floor window. It obviously wasn't coming. But still Pippa leaned forward in her wheelchair, pulling the curtain aside and remained focused. She rubbed vaguely at the band of mould under the ledge. Fingered the edge of the damp peeling wallpaper. Every time a vehicle pulled into the litter-strewn car park at the base of the tower block, she felt a moment's hope.

'Ring them again, Kim,' she pleaded.

Kim urged patience. Something must have gone wrong. Give them a bit longer. She'd just go and make another cuppa, then see where they stood. She climbed over the packing boxes which were piled up across their cramped flat. Each carefully labelled. For the lounge. Or for bedroom. Lamps – fragile. Books.

'Supposed to be here at 9am. It's nearly 12 all ready. Bloody ridiculous …' muttered Pippa.

Kim went into the kitchen but did not make the tea. She sat with her head in her hands. Trying to stop it exploding. There was no way out of this now. Everything had gone too far. Her world was enveloped in darkness. If only she could turn the clocks back two years. Before the accident. That bastard drunkard who smashed his car into Pippa as she crossed the road. She could still see the massive lump of car, squashing sylph-like Pippa. A sledge hammer cracking a peanut.

He'd got four years in jail. Pippa got a lifetime in a wheelchair.

Life was good before then. Yes, they were living in a grotty council block. But they had been saving up to buy a decent place. Still in Kings Heath, of course, but round the corner a bit. Perhaps Bank Street. They learned to cope with the constantly broken lift which always took ages to mend. Before quickly breaking down again. Pippa joked that she was glad they hadn't got a garden as they would never get the weeding done. The constant loud music from downstairs didn't matter too much. They were both out at work all day. And out again most evenings. Pippa was a fitness instructor at the local gym. Loved it. Not fabulous pay, but enough. Kim worked in the library. On a basic grade, but chances of promotion. Contented.

Living in Kings Heath was great. Lots of lesbians living locally. So much going on. Live music at the Kitchen Garden café, or The Hare and Hounds. Local musicians such as Steve Ajao. Women's rounders teams in Kings Heath Park. Painting classes at Cartlands tea rooms. Pink picnics in Highbury Park. Dyke's football at Cannon Hill. *Living the dream.*

Everything changed when Pippa was knocked over.

They had been busy all week attending International Women's Day events. They loved the photographic exhibition by Ming de Nasty. Original. Different to anything they had seen before. Pippa imagined buying a decent camera and trying to emulate the work. The ghost story night was a fabulous evening. Hanging on to each other and screaming with exaggerated fear. Women in theatre productions, showing the talents of local actors. Communal vegetarian breakfasts where they chewed cold sausages and planned the future. The craft fair in Tindall Street where they bought rare CDs and dream catchers.

It was on leaving the disco at the Hare and Hounds that it happened …

They were crossing the road when Kim realised she had dropped her keys on the pavement. Taking six steps back to retrieve them probably saved her life.

Crash. Crunch. Crumpled. Cacophony of screams.

After Pippa was discharged from hospital things became unbearable. Almost everything in her life evaporated.

Job. Money. Interests. Independence.

Slowly the new picture was revealed. And it was not pretty. There was a long waiting list for accessible housing with the council. Usually in grim areas where she did not want to live. Depression turned to lethargy. Black clouds hung over her. Friends visited at first. But didn't invite her out any more. Nights out for them were to let their hair down. Who would want to push the wheelchair round a pub or theatre? And, God forbid, supposing she wanted to go to the loo?

Kim converted from lover to carer. Working all day then coming home to cook. A cleaner was out of the question now that they had so little income. She did it all. Knowing that if it was, she who had been disabled, Pippa would have made a better job of it. Frustrated. Angry. Survivor's guilt.

It was Pippa who was disabled. Kim was paralysed.

Pippa watched Kim change from a laughing extrovert, life and soul of the party, into an anxious and exhausted shadow. She tried to ask for as little help as possible. Never mentioned that her bum was sore, or that she could scream at the sight of yet another ready meal. Kim was doing her best. She knew this. And she watched Kim's happiness drain away. Pippa had gone from being a fitness freak with a toned body, to a disabled woman who was piling on the pounds. It was hard to be enthusiastic about nothing. She reflected that if Kim had met her for the first time that day, they would not have become partners.

How were they going to manage? The useless lifts meant it was often impossible for Pippa to get out in her wheelchair. Then in desperation at the broken lifts, they hatched a plan. Kim bounced her in the wheelchair down the twelve flights of stairs. Trampolining down the stairwell turned out to be fun. Both enjoyed the thrill of it. Kim kept screaming that she was about to let go of the wheelchair. Pippa guffawed in response and hid her eyes in mock terror. They were shrieking with laughter by the time they reached the ground floor. At last, they could pop round to the local pub for a pint. A bit of normality.

They sat in the pub and drank their pints. Just like they used to. The good old days. Strangers raised their glasses in toast. Old faces came over to say hello.

Kim sat with her arm around Pippa. She felt like her lover again. And wondered again if sex might be possible now.

'Bloody good fun,' laughed Pippa, on leaving the pub. 'Must do it again some time …'

It wasn't quite so funny trying to get back upstairs at the end of their night out. Kim couldn't work out quite how to bounce the wheelchair back upstairs. Three pints of Guinness did not help clear thinking. Trying to get help, she approached neighbouring flats. Kim discovered that most people didn't answer their doorbells after dark. When she did eventually speak to someone, their bad back meant they couldn't help. As a last resort Kim thought of a muscular builder who lived round the corner. She had only spoken to him a couple of times but … He begrudgingly helped them. It took over an hour for the two of them to drag Pippa, in her wheelchair, back upstairs. Apart from the grunts and occasional swear words, all three were silent. Eventually they reached their front door.

'That was a fucking stupid thing to do,' the builder told Kim.

In bed that night, they huddled together. Thinking of a way to enjoy life more. This glum flat with its pathetic lift system was the cause of the problems. They decided they needed to buy a ground floor flat or bungalow. But how? Somehow, they would get the money together. Get a mortgage. The trip to the estate agents was an eye-opener. They were shocked at the price of flats. Bungalows completely out of the question.

Seeing Pippa's disappointment Kim determined to protect her. Get her the life she deserved. She knew she needed to get a promotion with a big pay rise. Sooner rather than later. The deputy librarian's job advertised at Bournville library paid a lot more.

'We can't do it,' whispered Pippa. 'Don't worry ...'

'Just watch me,' answered Kim. She would prove she could provide for the woman she loved.

Her interview went well, but she didn't get the job. Not enough experience. No qualifications in librarianship. She so much wanted to see Pippa happy that she lied. Told her she had got the job. Became convinced that she would be successful at the next try. It was worth this small fib to see her beaming face. Kim hadn't seen her look so happy since ...

They went through the motions of choosing a flat. A lovely ground floor flat with a garden on Wake Green Road. Pippa would be able to go into the garden while Kim was at work. Perhaps they could have barbecues. Invite their old mates round. Get some raised beds so Pippa could grow stuff. The owner was delighted when they said they were interested. With no property to sell it made them perfect buyers. Kim felt sad when the seller started to offer to leave furniture which they might want. Guilty.

Kim couldn't stall for much longer when Pippa started egging her to put in an offer to the estate agents. She said it would be just the job. *Living the dream*. An easy walk for Kim to Moseley village. Near the 50-bus stop for her work … And no bloody lifts …

The fantasy began. There were no new opportunities for promotion. The estate agent had actually laughed when she asked what kind of mortgage she could get on her current salary. At first it was easy to persuade Pippa that there had been a delay on the sale. Blaming problems further up the chain. Then she played out the deceit of working her notice. Eventually she had given Pippa a flat-moving date. This date had arrived.

But not the removal van.

Since the accident, Helen, Pippa's friend from work, called in to see her a couple of times. Brought her magazines and chocolates. Didn't come often. Such a drag getting up the five flights of stairs, never knowing who you might meet on the stairway. The dealers didn't bother her. It was men like the bloke who turned and followed her up to the flat, asking her how much she charged, that put her off.

And really, they didn't usually find much to talk about these days. Pippa's world had become so small. Helen was excited to hear about the move. Thought it would be great for both of them. Delighted that Kim had gained the promotion needed to fund the mortgage. Disability allowance for Pippa didn't go far. She offered to bring them a meal round to their new home on the day of removal.

Next time Helen visited would be her last. She asked Pippa if the move had fallen through. Said she was surprised to see the flat they were buying still had a For Sale notice up.

'Lazy bloody estate agents,' said Kim. 'God knows what they do to earn their fees.'

As evening approached, Pippa turned away from the window.

'We're not moving, are we?' she asked. Averted her gaze.

'Don't be daft ...' said Kim.

As Pippa glanced again into the darkening night, Kim crept up behind her. Pippa turned and her eyes widened. She saw in Kim's eyes the loss and hopelessness she felt herself. Nodded. For an eternity Kim pressed on her throat. She was surprised at how little resistance Pippa offered. Did not even raise her arms to protect herself. Almost as though she was expecting it. Almost as though she wanted it. She finally stopped breathing.

'Sorry my love,' Kim said, and kissed her.

Afterwards Kim sat with Pippa's body. Brushed her hair and stroked her face. Kissed her on the mouth and the throat. Kim laid her on the floor, covering her up to her armpits with her favourite patchwork throw. She'd made it at a craft group. On her head she placed the floral crown which she used to wear at music festivals. Bought it at Womad a few years ago. Lit the patchouli candle Helen had bought her the previous Christmas. Placed it on the floor beside her. Next to the framed photo of them both dancing at the Women's Day disco. In another life.

The police arrived quickly. Four officers. Burst into the room. Then stood silently , surveying the murder scene.

'What?' asked the Sergeant. 'What…?'

'I just …' started Kim. 'I just couldn't bear to disappoint her.'

Claire and Gina — 1997

This one looked promising. Said quite clearly that they wanted a vegetarian who liked hill-walking. Hopefully she would have more luck this time. The soulmates ads, in the Guardian, were quite limited. Few women looking for women. Curled up on the sofa, Gina re-read it. Yes; she would take a risk with this one. Hoped she wasn't another nutter like the last couple.

Some months ago, she'd exchanged letters with a woman called Naomi. Sounded lovely. Then followed a few phone calls. Finally, the decision to meet up. Gina finished it before they actually met. Was put off when Naomi wanted to check that she actually owned her own house. Said she was sick of living in rented property.

Another woman responded enthusiastically to her all her suggestions of hill-walking. But then admitted that she preferred staying home to watch the television. Started reeling of a list of her favourite soaps. Then there was the one who still lived at home with her mum, and sounded suspiciously young. *Not going there.* Eventually she did meet up with an attractive hill-walker who seemed promising. Until it became apparent that she was still in love with her ex.

But this one sounded reasonable. Gina found her favourite line in Claire's letter.

I'll race you to the top of Snowdon.

The smile stretched across Gina's face. She liked the energy portrayed. And the self-confidence. Looking at the photo she could see a small, slim woman. Pretty fair hair tied back in a low pony tail. Azure eyes. Fine cheek bones. She realised that she had been staring at the photo for several minutes. Claire was attractive and athletic looking. And yes; vegetarian. Perfect.

Gina studied herself in the mirror. Would need to get her own wavy red hair trimmed. It was always a bit wild. Not everyone liked that. She might pop to the dentists to get her teeth cleaned. Wanted to make a good impression. Looking at the letter again she grinned before taking out her own notepaper.

Dear Claire,

So glad you contacted me. Would love to race you to the summit of Snowdon. Last one up buys the coffees.

Name the date
Gina.

They met, of course, at the Fox. Strapline – The little gay bar with the big gay heart. Strange that they had never met before. A regular stomping ground for them both. But then, there were always so many women crushed in there. Hilli was behind the bar as always. Serving the drinks with a smile. Gave Gina a wink. They chose to splash out and have a cocktail. Celebrating their first date. Both opted for the 'Foxy lady.' Grabbing their drinks they decided on a game of pool to break the ice. So much easier talking to a stranger when you can avoid eye contact. And pause before replying. Gives you chance to have a good look at each other as well.

The back room of the Fox housed the pool table. On the dark wooden chairs around the sides were perched drinkers and spectators. Most were nursing a pint of Guiness. On the walls were pictures of iconic women. Most were trying to remember who they were. The ceiling was covered with hanging baseball caps which regulars brought back from their holidays. It was a tradition and a talking point for new-comers. People were calling out advice to players.

Their game was over quickly when Gina accidently potting the black on her second shot. Cheers from the audience as she held her head in her hands. Laughing, Claire suggested they went through to the beer garden. Gina realised that Claire was tougher than she looked. Belonged to a running group. Played football. Had taken part in a relay channel swim. Gina flinched. Yes; Claire would almost certainly beat her to the summit of Snowdon. But Gina would put up a fight. She looked forward to it and grinned.

'Did you go on the AIDs march last December?' asked Claire. 'I might have seen you there.'

Gina nodded. Conversation flowed. They had lots in common. Claire sat back and ran her fingers through her loose blonde hair. She held eye contact with Gina. Tipped her glass into her mouth, and watched her as she slowly sipped. Crossing her legs she edged closer. Gina leaned forward. Gently touched her arm.

'Fancy doing the Karaoke with me?' asked Claire.

'It's called the Foxeoke on Fridays,' laughed Gina.

Grabbing the two mics, they were soon singing along to 'I am what I am …' giggling and falling onto each other when they messed up the words. Egged on by the noisy drinkers. Some-one offered to buy them a drink.

Holding hands afterwards , they moved towards the main bar , finding a stool.

'Did you know …?' asked Claire, before noticing a woman in the corner of the room. 'Oh, bloody hell , no.'

Gina realised that a stranger was now glaring at them both. Spiky black hair with faux dreadlocks. Brightly coloured patchwork trousers. The woman picked up her pint, marched across to them, and tipped it over Claire's head. A frothy brown waterfall.

'Bitch,' she said, before storming out of the pub.

Claire stood still, with eyes tightly shut, as the beer soaked her shirt and Levi jeans. New on today. She watched the departing woman in silence. Then brushed her sticky hair away from her face.

'What?' gasped Gina. 'What on earth?'

'Bloody hell,' sighed Claire. 'I'll have to go home and get changed.' She looked around at concerned drinkers and waved away offers of help.

'Sorry, Gina. Coming with me?' she asked. 'This is a long story …'

Gina hesitated. What was going on here? Who was that nutty woman? This was seriously weird. Gina realised she would need to be reckless or stupid to go back to a stranger's house, within a few hours of meeting her. But she grabbed her jacket and followed Claire's wet footprints out of the pub They flagged down a taxi. This date was turning out to be quite exciting.

Claire's small house on Balaclava Road was cold and dark when they arrived. She switched on the lights and lit the gas fire. Then, asking Gina to wait in the sitting room, she went for a quick shower and change of clothes. Gina was greeted by a Border Terrier wagging its tail. Its bone-shaped label said 'Brillo.' Gina laughed as he jumped on her knee and licked her face. Then rolled onto its back asking for tummy rubs. Wonderful welcome.

Claire returned with wet hair and wearing tartan pyjamas. She made the coffee with a sigh. Said she knew the date had gone badly. Really awkward start. Such a shame as they had been having a great time. Hadn't they? Appreciated Gina coming back to talk it through. Claire took a deep breath before recounting the story.

The barmy woman was called Zoe. Claire first met her at a crowded café when she asked if she could sit at her table. Zoe, it seemed, was a sad woman. Her girlfriend dumped her recently and she couldn't get over it. Wanted to get out and start mixing again, but didn't have the confidence. Before they parted, Claire agreed that Zoe could go with her and her friends to the women's disco the following week. A kind gesture. *No good deed goes unpunished.*

At the disco, Claire introduced other friends to

Zoe. They were all having a great time, dancing and drinking. Zoe spent the evening socialising with them. All went well until a woman asked Claire for the last, smoochy dance. Arms around each other, stroking each other. A nibble of the ear.

Then Zoe sprang across at the couple and whacked Claire across the back of the head.

'How dare you ask me out on a date, then treat me like this?' yelled Zoe, before running from the hall sobbing.

'Bloody hell,' said Gina. 'Terrifying. She must be bonkers.'

It can be a problem for lesbians when they make new female friends. Are they just mates, or is this the prelude to a relationship?

Claire continued with the saga, whilst gulping her coffee. As she knew where Zoe lived, she waited for her to come home from work. Apologised for the misunderstanding and explained that she just wanted friendship. Zoe had been calm and asked her in for a cuppa. They agreed that it would be good to be friends.

Gina sipped her coffee and considered all this. She looked around at the ordinariness of the room. Red velour sofa. Coffee table with mug stains, and an old newspaper. Overflowing bin on the hearth. What didn't make sense was that Zoe was still angry with her. And how did she know where Claire was tonight?

Apparently, Zoe often followed Claire. Never really accepted the rejection. Would just appear unexpectedly. Once followed her round Woolworths, when she was buying a CD. Ingenue. Claire guessed that if she ignored her, she would soon tire of this stupidity. But sadly … She also appeared at a meditation group, and once at a café where Claire was eating with her sister. Usually sat staring at her. Other times ignored her, as though it was a coincidence. Things progressed. Claire discovered that Zoe was hinting to people they were a couple. Nothing direct; just bashful silences when people asked her, averted eyes, smiles … The Fox was the obvious place for her to try next.

When Claire paused, Gina put her arms around her and stroked her face. She had been through so much. Then came the kiss. A special kiss. Then; would Gina like to stay the night? Gina explained that she made a rule never to have sex on a first date. But would love to stay the night as it was getting late. She snuggled into bed with Claire and Brillo. Soon she was breaking her own rules. A tsunami washed over her before she fell asleep.

A week later they were at Cannon Hill Park, enjoying a drink outside the MAC. Gina was enjoying hearing about Claire's past escapades. How she once got stuck in the middle of a burning field in Ireland, when trekking the Ring of Kerry. She ended up missing a plane in Italy as she was too engrossed in a new girlfriend to hear the announcement. And embarrassingly ended up on a blind date with an ex-teacher.

Gina embellished a few of her own stories. She once left a café without paying, ran for miles chased by the owners … Paid a fortune for a pair of sunglasses which she left in a hut half way up a Swiss mountain …

Gina kept throwing the ball for Brillo. He loved chasing it; leaping in the air to catch it. Enjoyed the applause. Then ran back with it, wanting it to be thrown again. The Canada geese in the lake were honking. The summer sun was fading on the evening. Then Gina threw the ball too hard, and watched as it plopped into the lake. Her laughter soon stopped, when she saw Brillo chase it, into the water. Floundering around he was gasping and wide-eyed.

'He can't swim,' shouted Claire.

They both leapt to their feet in time to see Zoe appear from nowhere. She hurtled towards the lake and jumped in. Grabbing Brillo, she picked him up and kissed him. Then carried him back to Claire.

'Be more careful with him,' shouted Zoe, before hugging Brillo and walking away.

Gina and Claire silently watched her walk away. Dripping wet. Reminiscent of the scene in the Fox a few weeks ago. They were relieved that she had rescued him. But where the hell had Zoe appeared from? How long had she been watching them? Gina shivered although it was a warm evening. She stood up and watched Zoe walk back to the car park. Got into a distinctive red 2CV. Drove away without looking back.

'No idea she was here,' said Gina. 'What a nut job …'

'I've got used to it …' replied Claire.

'We need to do something about it …' started Gina.

Claire nodded.

They soon joined the book group at the home of Claire's friend, Parmjit. Lovely to meet on autumn evenings. Discussed the book, 'Trumpet' by Jackie Kay. They were all fans of hers. Some had been to a recent poetry workshop she had run in Ledbury. Inspiring! Parmjit had a cat called Mopsy. Otherwise,

Brillo could have attended. Mopsy had only lived with her for a few months. Got her about the same time that Brillo went to live with Claire. Parmjit remembered when Brillo moved in. Took him a while to settle in as he was anxious. Lucky for him that Claire had agreed to take him on. His previous owner had lost her job and could no longer afford to keep him.

Gina suggested walking over the Malvern Hills at the weekend. Get some practice in before heading to Snowdon. Sunday was fine and they marched towards British camp. . For a ten-year-old dog Brillo was sprightly and energetic, racing ahead of them. They sat on the earthworks at the Iron Age fort, enjoying the view. A giddy perspective to look down on the tiny people at the reservoir. Strange in such an open landscape for there to be no trees. Gina was relieved that it meant there was nowhere for anyone to hide. She stroked Claire's hair and smiled. They sauntered back, holding hands. Sat outside St Anne's Well café eating veggie burgers. The chef gave Brillo a sausage which he woolfed down, before falling asleep and snoring. Claire fetched them both glasses of water from the spring, and Brillo lapped from his bowl.

'Apparently Saint Anne was the maternal grand-mother of Christ,' said Gina. 'I doubt she ever visited this well, though.'

They giggled. It was a cheery place. Locals passed and spoke to them. Walkers carried rucksacks and some used poles. The café owner came out and spoke at length about the weather, the state of the nation, and how his best friend just lost his license. They ordered chocolate cake and another pot of tea.

'Which rescue did you get Brillo from?' asked Gina.

'She came from a friend,' replied Claire. ' I love this cake?'

Arriving back at Claire's house, they noticed the red 2CV parked opposite. They hurried to open Claire's front door. Zoe rushed up and asked if she could stroke Brillo for just a minute. Brillo pulled towards her and clearly enjoyed it.

'Now, stay away!' shouted Claire.

Six months rushed by. Claire and Gina agreed that they were an item. At some stage, maybe next year, they might move in together. They didn't want to rush it.

'Remember that old joke?' asked Gina. 'What does a lesbian take on her second date?'

'Everything she owns,' laughed Claire.

Gina worked in the offices of Safe-homes. Providing accommodation for vulnerable people. One Tuesday she was walking through reception, when Zoe approached her.

'I want to apply for a flat,' Zoe said.

'Go to the reception desk and give them your details,' snapped Gina, rushing past her.

Later she looked at Zoe's application. Having been evicted from her flat, she was sleeping in her car. Couldn't face the hostels as they were too dangerous. Receiving support from mental health services. Explained a bit about her odd behaviour.

Claire and Gina went to Brighton for a weekend. Stayed in a lovely Georgian guesthouse near the sea front. Strolled along the pier. Wobbled along the stoney beach. Enjoyed the gay bars in Kemp town. Ate at the vegetarian restaurants and cafes. Sitting in Terra Terra, they looked at the posh menu. Paul McCartney was rumoured to eat here. There was no sign of him then. Ordered the rosti spinach as everything else looked weird. Gulped at the price tag. Got up early next day to skinny dip on the Nudist beach. Brillo loved running into the sea. They both kept close to him to make sure he didn't get swept out. Later, in the hotel, they bathed and dried him.

'When Brillo fell in the lake last week, 'began Gina' 'Zoe was very concerned.'

Claire continued towelling Brillo dry.

'Had she met him before?' asked Gina.

Claire explained that actually, Brillo used to belong to Zoe. She had rehomed him when Zoe told her she could no longer afford to keep him. Gina took some time to digest this information. She frowned and stroked him. When Claire had gone to Zoe's house, the day after the incident at the disco, she was upset. Zoe was crying about having to give up her dog. She'd lost her job so couldn't afford to keep her flat or dog. Everything was going wrong for her at the same time. Claire jumped at the chance to have Brillo. Zoe was distraught about letting him go, but agreed it was the best thing for him. She carried on sobbing, heaving and sighing. Claire decided to cheer her up.

'I broke my own rules,' Claire said. 'It was only the once.'

'You mean you …?' asked Gina.

'Yes,' answered Claire. 'You know, just a quick comfort shag.'

Gina gulped. Claire explained that Zoe knew from the off that there was no chance of a relation-ship. In fact, told her to keep away as it might upset

Brillo if he saw Zoe again. Gina's eyes widened as she stared at Claire.

'But then she started following me,' continued Claire. 'Became a bloody nuisance ...'

'Claire,' started Gina, wringing her hands, 'I can't get my head around ...'

Claire explained that she had never felt anything but pity for Zoe. Was now being punished for her kindness. She just needed to shake her off ...

They drove back to Kings Heath in silence. Gina was struggling to make sense of it all. Stared out of the window. Shook her head. Stared at Claire then looked away. When they pulled up outside Claire's house, the red 2CV was parked on the opposite side of the road.

'Right,' shouted Claire. 'I'm sick of her fucking everything up for me. I'm gonna have a word.'

'No,' said Gina, pressing her hand on her arm. 'Stay here. I'll go.'

Claire punched the steering wheel, then threw herself back into her seat.

Gina walked over to the red car, opened the passenger seat and sat down.

'Hi Zoe,' she said. 'Come to my office tomorrow. I might be able to offer you a small flat. Over in Quinton.'

Zoe nodded.

'And,' she added, 'I'll help you to get your dog back.'

Cheryl and Anne — 2001

Cheryl hadn't wanted to slap a student before, but this time she was forced to leave the classroom to stop herself. As she stormed out the kids cheered. Harry Bradshaw stood on his desk, punching the air with his fist and laughing. Everyone got up to admire the stream of piss running down the back wall and onto the polished wooden floors. The head-teacher rushed in, and restored order.

By 8pm, when Anne arrived home, Cheryl had drunk a bottle of wine and uncorked a second. She lay on the sofa gazing at the ceiling. Her face was blotchy and wet. She hadn't changed out of her work clothes. Anne looked expectantly at the dining table, which was not set. Nothing was cooking in the oven. No welcoming smells of supper.

'What are we eating?' she asked.

'Fuck all,' replied Cheryl. 'Unless you order us a takeaway.'

Hastily prepared cheese sandwiches and a packet of crisps, eaten in silence. They went to bed and slept back-to-back.

'Thanks for your concern,' sobbed Cheryl.

'We've all got our problems,' answered Anne, staring at the wall.

Awaking in the early hours, Anne replayed the events of the last couple of years. Why was she in such a bloody mess? She and Cheryl had bought this house twenty years ago. Her mother, who hated her, had helpfully popped her clogs and left Anne a sizeable legacy. This meant that Anne could also set up her own accountancy firm in Kings Heath. She always hated having a boss, and now she was top dog. Never any shortage of work.

With Cheryl's teacher's salary as well, they had bought this five-bedroomed house on Oxford Road. The envy of most of the local dykes. Not many couples in their thirties lived so comfortably. Holidays abroad and lots of theatre trips.

Anne turned on her side and stroked Cheryl's sleeping body. Then crept downstairs to her office. She re-read the account; the details were still the same. Her pension pot accumulated over 30 years was emptied; there was nothing left. Nothing to show for it. Leaning her head on her forearms she fell asleep.

Over the years, Cheryl enjoyed teaching less. She never gained the promotions she sought. The kids were more badly behaved every new term. The parents were increasingly hostile. What seemed an exciting challenge thirty years ago was now a wearying irritation. As for the pointless school inspections? Oh, please …! Long ago she had woken each morning with excitement, looking ahead to her plans for the pupils. Imagined how their lives would be expanded. Now she dreaded the swearing and threats. The look of disgust from the head teacher when she asked for help with classroom management.

Anne set off for her run at 6am. Ran through Highbury Park and sat in the wooded area. Remembering the first picnic she shared with Debbie. Here, under this very oak tree. Early spring and the daffodils were just peeping through. New beginnings as the leaves unfurled. Fresh. Hopeful. They were out of sight. She was aware that Debbie was over 20 years her junior. Felt unworthy of her. When they had sex for the first time, under cover of the nearby rhododendron bush, she was overwhelmed. Anne hadn't experienced such passion for years. Then they did it again, making Anne late back for her afternoon client. Her secretary commented that she looked flushed.

Returning home at 8am, she found Cheryl sitting in her dressing gown, drinking coffee.

'I've rung in sick,' said Cheryl. 'We need to talk.'

'What? …' asked Anne.

Cheryl stood up and stroked Anne's face. Then kissed her lightly on the lips. Just a second's brush against her. Anne shivered.

'You know how rotten things are at school for me …' began Cheryl, flopping down on the sofa. 'I can't do it. They are absolute little bleeders…'

'Only a few more years, 'replied Anne. 'You're coming up 56 and then …'

Cheryl banged her coffee cup down. She crossed the room and peered out into the garden. Autumn was beautiful. The leaves on their oak trees were already turning brown. Ready to rest. She could sense their weariness after blooming all year. Soon they would make a gorgeous carpet across the lawn. Knowing their work was done.

'I've given my notice in,' she blurted out. 'That's it!'

Anne's face was a wax mask. She gripped the mug tighter, and joined Cheryl at the window. She, too peered out into the garden. Autumn was a defeated time of year. Everything gave up. The once-beautiful flowers were shrivelling. Out-lived their usefulness. The lawn had scattered holes where the squirrels had dug it up. Even the water-but was overflowing and muddy. All ruined.

'Don't be silly ...' Anne said.

'Too late; it's done,' said Cheryl. 'Most women have months off work for maternity leave. I've never had any of that. Never had a break ...'

'Hang on, there's something ...' started Anne.

The women locked eyes.

How could she explain it to Cheryl? Even as she rehearsed the words in her head it sounded bonkers.

'Look, love, 'said Anne, 'Got two meetings this morning. Must dash. Fancy meeting me at Manic Organic for lunch?'

Striding to her office, Anne shook her head. All this chaos for 15 months of ... of what? Sex? Excitement? Being able to imagine she was twenty years younger? Stupidity.

Cheryl looked more relaxed when she came into the café, where Anne had already ordered their coffees.

'Should do this more often,' she smiled. 'Doctor's signed me off sick for my notice period. So, I'm free.' She spread her arms out and then hugged herself. 'Never going back again.'

Anne had chosen the most secluded part of the tea garden for them to sit. Needed to get on with it and tell Cheryl about their situation. Had no idea how she would react to the news, but she had to know. Urgently. *Do it now, Anne.* She felt pressure in her head. Pounding in her ears. Her throat closed as she tried to drink her coffee. Confessing the affair was the least of it.

The waiter carried their salads to the table. Freshly baked bread. Olives. As she placed them on the table, the manager ran out into the garden after her.

'Twin towers in America… Planes crashed into them … people jumping from windows to escape the flames …'

'They think it was deliberate …'

'Christ!' shouted Cheryl' How bloody awful.'

No-one saw this coming!

They ate their lunch and the conversation was taken over by the atrocities in America. Other customers joined them, shaking and considering what it would all mean. Anne said nothing. Wrapped in her own misery, she found it hard to care about strangers across the pond. Her own life was about to explode. No energy left for this.

Cheryl wanted to go home. Said she needed to fill in forms for work. Bye-bye little brats. Good luck to whoever gets my job. You'll need it. Hearing about the twin towers burning reminded her how precious each day was.

After a long afternoon, when Anne had difficulty concentrating on her clients, she trudged home. Only a 20-minute walk. She wished it was longer.

She walked up their drive, past the dying lavender bushes which she had planted a few years ago. Saw the lamps glowing through the window. Watched Cheryl setting the table for supper. Entering the hallway, she glanced at the framed photos. Pictures of them both at Pride many years ago. Laughing. Wearing daft hats with rainbows. Drinking from bottles. Arms around each other. How long ago was this? A hundred years?

Cheryl had seen her arrive and was all ready serving lasagne and salad. Anne sat down and tore off a piece of garlic bread. Dipped it in her steaming dish.

'This is the best day of for ages,' said Cheryl. 'To celebrate I've opened that bottle of sparkly that we were saving for Christmas.'

101

Anne's eyes were fixed on the place mats. This was too much. If only she could blame someone else. Anyone. But the treachery was all hers.

'We aren't watching the news again tonight,' said Cheryl. 'Can't bear all that awful stuff in America. Nothing gonna spoil ...'

'I have got to tell you now,' whispered Anne.

Cheryl's smile left her face. She tilted her head to one side and looked at Anne.

'It's a long story, but you need to know, 'she began. 'What I've done is unforgiveable.'

'What?' said Cheryl. 'Nothing's that bad, love.'

'Worse,' sighed Anne.

Cheryl sat in silence, taking gulps of champagne. Topping it up, as Anne explained. It had all been stupid. She would never forgive herself. Didn't expect Cheryl to.

Cheryl whispered, 'What the bloody hell ...?'

Yes; an affair. Yes; it was definitely over. Started as a silly flirtation. Went on for a couple of months. Or a bit longer. No; she meant nothing to her. Just sex.

'Just sex?' shouted Cheryl. 'You haven't touched me for months!'

She threw her glass across the room and they both watched motionless as it smashed and the drink slithered down the wall.

Anne couldn't explain it to herself. Why she had got involved. She and Cheryl had chugged along together for over twenty years. No big arguments. Smashing holidays. Trips to the theatre. And love. They always supported each other. Hugged each other when their parents died. Looked after each other when they were ill. Took turns at the housework ...

No excitement.

Can women expect passion when they are staring old age in the face?

'I want to punch you on the nose,' shouted Cheryl. 'I hate you.'

'I can't say I blame you, 'whispered Anne.

'That bloody kid at school pissed all over the wall, and you have pissed all over me.'

Anne became silent as Cheryl sat sobbing. If some-one else had done this she would call them a fool. It wasn't clear now when the sex became a relationship. When Debbie made it clear she wanted more. Anne struggled. She loved Cheryl and didn't want to leave their home. But she needed Debbie as well. Debbie, who was living in a rented flat across the city.

The plan evolved. Anne would remortgage their house and use the equity to buy a house for Debbie. £120,000. It was easy to forge Cheryl's signature. They chose a property in Reddings Road. Nice little semi. Good garden. Just right. Close enough for Anne to pop in whenever, but unlikely that Cheryl would see her. The house was put in Debbie's name to prove Anne's commitment. They would change it to joint names when Anne felt ready to separate from Cheryl. On the day their offer for the house was accepted Anne took the day off work. She and Debbie spent the time in bed.

'How did I get this far in life without you?' sighed Anne.

'There's more…' stammered Anne, looking at Cheryl.
'More women? ' screamed Cheryl. 'What the …'

Anne was Chartered Accountant. Used to noticing if things weren't honest and straightforward. So why hadn't she noticed all the tell-tale signs before? On the day that the contracts were exchanged, the tectonic plates shifted. The solicitor had handed Debbie the keys and they popped out for a celebratory drink. As it was Cheryl's birthday, Anne wanted to spend the evening with her. They arranged to meet the next day, after work, at the new house. Debbie booked the removal van for the following morning.

Yes; she had booked the removal van to empty her rented flat in Erdington. But when Anne called round next day, she shook her head when she saw there was no furniture was being unpacked at Reddings Road. And no Debbie Had the removal van been delayed? It was 6pm so should have been here hours ago. Anne drove at speed to Debbie's home address.

She peered through the ground floor window of what had been Debbie's flat. They had spent many secret hours here. The lounge was barren. Marks on the carpets in front of where the sofa had been. Oblong grey marks on the walls showing that pictures had been removed. A knot in her stomach. A lump in her throat. Where was Debbie? They must have passed each other on spaghetti junction. She rushed back to Reddings Road, covering the eight miles at speed.

Pulling up outside the empty house, Anne braced herself. No lights on. No movement. No-one there. Her face was rigid. Her heart was racing. Her stomach rumbling. She hadn't. of course, got a key She'd never thought of it when the bunch of keys was handed to Debbie. Driving back to Erdington, she arrived at the home of Debbie's landlord. He recognised her.

'Hi. My mate Debbie, left some things …' began Anne. 'Can't find the post it note where she wrote her new address down…'

The landlord had not been given a forwarding address. Cheryl had said something about moving to Sheffield. Left the place lovely and clean. And not pinched anything; not like the last tenant. If Anne knew anyone who wanted to rent …

The words fell out reluctantly. Anne's voice was strangled as she explained. Cheryl's eyes grew wider as her distress increased. Anne forced herself to empty the whole heap of misery onto Cheryl's lap. *Keep going … keep going … tell her the lot …*

When she finally fell silent, Cheryl sprang up and slapped her across the back of her head. Then started weeping again. She hadn't seen this coming. She grabbed her coat and car keys, and ran out of the door. Anne watched her drive away at speed. Into the darkness.

Cheryl parked in Cannon Hill car park. The Arts Centre was busy with people going to see a film. Or having a drink at the bar. Happy people. People whose partner had not just wrecked both their lives. *No fool like an old fool.* She bought a glass of wine in a plastic tumbler and went to sit next to the lake. Music came from the bar. *Girls just wanna have fun.*

Which was worse? That Anne had been having an affair, or that she had re-mortgaged their house? Forged her signature for God's sake! She could get her sent to jail! Had a good mind to. That would teach her. And why was she off with that bloody hussy, Debbie, when she could have been home with her? Her tears mixed with the dregs of her wine.

Staring across the lake, she peered at the waning crescent of the moon. Another few days and it would be done ... All that brightness, shining and golden, gradually disappearing. And it had been a glorious moon.

She noticed an old woman, wearing only a nightie and slippers, scurrying along the side of the lake. Rambling something about getting home. Paused at the edge of the lake and peered into the dark waters. Heard a shout of 'Mum, wait ...' Then two women caught up with her and ushered her away from the lake. They spoke to her in calm voices, urging her to return home with them. They told her that her granny was waiting at home for her. Appeased, the confused woman allowed herself to be escorted away.

For Cheryl, this brought back memories of a few years ago, when she had lost her Mum, Sarah.

During her last year Sarah had lived with her and Anne. Dementia increasing, until she didn't know who either of them were. Cheryl had never wanted to be a nurse. Was horrified by incontinence and food slopped everywhere. Impatient with being told by Sarah that she had no right to hold her here, against her will. Frustrated at the limitations it brought to their lives. Observing her dignified mum farting loudly and shreiking with glee. It was all too much for her.

Cheryl was surprised to watch Anne nurturing Sarah. Insisting that she be the one to lose sleep when Sarah was wandering round the house in the early hours. Anne was the one who bathed her and changed her soiled pads. It was Anne who pureed her food to make it easier to swallow. It was Anne who took annual leave when the carers let them down … Cheryl couldn't face any of it. Was ashamed to feel the relief that flooded her when Sarah died.

Anne went to sit in the darkened garden after Cheryl left. Sat looking at the dying moon. *Like the moon, we must go through phases of emptiness to feel whole again.*

What would she have done if Cheryl had done all of this? Probably left her and never spoken to her again. Nothing could be undone. She leaned her head on the garden table and drifted off to sleep.

It was about 2am when Cheryl shook her awake. Sat down on the bench next to her.

Anne looked at her and said, 'I can never …'

'No, you can't,' snapped Cheryl. She peered around the garden as though expecting to find something hiding under one of the bushes. A young fox came towards them, cocking its head on one side, as though to ask why they hadn't put his food out tonight. 'I'm going to apply for some private teaching work. Personal tuition. Get this bloody mortgage paid off.'

Anne was silent and just raised her eyebrows.

'Every day, for the rest of our lives, you will treat me decently,' intoned Cheryl. 'Any stepping out of line and I will definitely strangle you. Definitely.'

Anne's face was wet, and she could only nod.

'Don't ever mention that stinking woman's name again,' she added.

Anne put her arm round Cheryl's shoulders and pulled her close. She stroked the side of her face. As she kissed her on the mouth, she cupped her breast and squeezed her nipple.

'Yes,' sobbed Cheryl. 'Maybe …'

Edith and Mary — 2003

She sat in the corner of her room in the faux-leather recliner. Crocheting a square of something, which would never be used. Threading the yarns, pink and blue, yellow and green. Sighing. Looking out of the window she saw that autumn was here. Brown leaves falling across the lawn. The sun low in the sky. Wind shaking the Rowan tree. It was no good; she would have to go out and say hello to the other residents. Make an effort to be sociable. Try to conquer the loneliness.

Edith wandered into the common room using her walking frame. It helped her to walk safely but it drummed home that unwelcome message. You are old. Disabled. Can't manage alone. The residents of Honeysuckle House gathered there when they became bored with their own company. Left their small rooms, with their nostalgic photos, and headed out to see who was there. The usual suspects were next to the window. Three of them reminiscing about the old days. The lives they left behind. Who they missed. And who they were glad to see the back of. She knew their stories by heart. But they had never heard hers. Or, just a sanitised version of it. Joining them she smiled, and knew they would not have been friends if they had met 30 years ago.

Rita pushed the trolley in, calling hello to everyone. Wearing her regulation blue uniform. And decidedly non-uniform long painted nails. Morning coffee was served. A choice of biscuits from the Fox's family assortment tin. Edith chose a custard cream and a malted milk. Didn't want to gain weight if she could help it. Her Les had always admired her slim shape. Not that he was here to see it now ... She watched as the carers started to assist the most disabled clients. Glad that she was still able to move around the place without much help.

When matron walked in with an unknown woman, they all looked around. A bit of excitement! Mary was introduced to them as the new girl. They all laughed at this oft-repeated joke. Presumably she would be taking Josephine's room. Never left much time between the funeral and the next admission. Matron beamed at them all as she explained that Mary would be staying for six weeks, while her at-home carer was off sick. This was a bit of a novelty for the residents as most of them didn't leave unless it was in a box.

Mary looked around the room, with her hands on the sides of her wheelchair. She didn't smile at anyone, but neither did she seem as dismayed as most new arrivals. Had the confidence of someone who knew this was temporary. Despite her drooping left arm, she looked fitter than most of them. Perhaps she had dementia? But usually, the ones who lost their marbles were housed in another wing. 'Gone to university' they said to each other, rolling their eyes. When someone's condition deteriorated to force the transfer.

Edith eyed Mary. Liked her stoicism. Something about her reminded her of her Les, bless him. A sense of determination. Not submission.

And Mary eyed Edith. A flicker of recognition in her eye. They held eye contact for a few seconds, and then Mary was wheeled away to unpack.

The dining room was pretty in a practical sort of way. Six round tables, each with six chairs. A wipe-clean table covering with a lacy floral pattern. Washable flooring. Pink checked curtains at the windows. Windows locked to only open six inches. Large pink paper napkins at every place. Supplemented by a kitchen roll in the centre of each table.

At lunch Edith sat in her usual place, next to Cynthia. The table with a good view of the garden. They both enjoyed watching the birds at the feeders. Today they could see blue tits and a blackbird. Commented that they hadn't seen a woodpecker for a while. But Cynthia thought she heard owls hooting this morning. Hoping one of the foxes would make an appearance.

Edith watched as Mary entered the room and was directed towards a table near the door.

'I'd rather sit at the table over there,' said Mary, indicating the empty place next to Edith. 'If you don't mind.' Then she spun her wheels, sending the wheelchair across the room at speed. It stopped abruptly and was manipulated into position. Here was a woman who wouldn't conform.

The five seated women inspected her with interest. She must be about their ages; 80's. Though Cynthia was nearer 90. Neatly cut short grey hair. Dark blue jumper. And the ubiquitous elastic-waisted black trousers. She returned their stares. Seemed especially interested in Edith, although she went round the table asking everyone's name. Leaving Edith until last.

'Yes,' she replied to Edith. 'I think I knew your husband. Les, wasn't it?'

The grandfather clock in the corner struck one.

'Lost him a while back, 'replied Edith, taking a bite of pork pie. 'To cancer.'

The talk moved on to how they had all ended up in this place, and who they had been before. Cynthia did paid work after marriage. She worked in the post office. At the counter. Complained that the men sitting next to her, doing the exact same job, earned more than her. When she questioned them about this, they explained that it was because the blokes had to pay for the girls when they went out on dates.

The others had all worked in factories, making ammunition for the war. Or grew vegetables on the farms in Shropshire. All part of the war effort. After 1945 the men came home. Or, some of them. Those who still had husbands went back home to their kitchens. Some relieved, but others regretful.

Mary was noticeably quiet. When pressed, she said she hadn't taken part in the war. Registered as a Conscientious Objector. She looked around to assess their responses. Didn't believe in wars and violence. It was just what the men at the top wanted. You know, those men who don't go to war themselves. A ripple of excitement flooded the group. Someone different here! How did she feel about hiding at home when their husbands were out at war, or making weapons in factories? And the women all doing their bit too.

'Well,' Mary replied, 'the fourteen days in Strangeways prison wasn't much fun.'

The women all leaned forward with wide eyes. Cynthia choked on her pickled onion and had to be patted on the back. Everyone was alert. Mary used to work in a shop before, but they sacked her when she became a CO.

'How did you get out of it?' asked Edith. 'We were all called up to do something.'

Mary had never married and was childless. So was called up for military service. Her refusal to engage in war work, in any way, lead her to the tribunal where she requested registration as a CO. An unfriendly bunch of bigwigs. She was asked why she wasn't a vegetarian if she was a pacifist. Told that the best thing she could do was to starve herself to death, leaving the sparse food rations for those who deserved them. During her stay in prison, the pastor berated her. Said that even God kills people. He kills us all in the end. But pastor couldn't answer when she asked why they were encouraged to pray for their enemies.

While Mary was recounting all this, Edith was transfixed. Something about this story rang a bell for her. She remembered her hubby, Les, saying he had met a CO. Felt he could understand her point of view. He had hated the war, and his job of making ammunition. But didn't have the courage … Felt it was a brave thing to do. Edith struggled to remember if Les had ever named the woman, and wasn't sure he had.

Dear Les. She missed him so much. Taken too soon. They'd never had any kids of course, with them both being women. So, no offspring to help in her old age. No nieces or nephews either. Some of the friends she had made in later years turned against her after he died. When they found out that Les was born female. A few stayed close to her. But as they were old and frail themselves, she had ended up coming here. Not that it was too bad. Just, not home. And, no Les …

Edith wasn't surprised when Mary popped into her room later, offering to share her chocolates. She stared as Mary sat in the armchair under her window. Didn't usually invite people into her room. What was Mary up to? She said she knew Les. How? And what exactly did she know about him? Was she here to humiliate her? Or bribe her? None of the other residents knew her secret. None of their business really.

There was just a brief mention in the paper, when he died, but not something that most people would notice.

Jackson Leslie, aka Les, died 28.06.1996. Missed by his dear friend Edith, and his mates at The Old Mo. Private funeral. Close friends only.

His old mate, Phil, from the darts group, has placed the obituary. Only a couple of months before he died himself. So, another one of her few remaining friends gone. And her bodged hip replacement and the wretched arthritis made it difficult to manage alone. So, she ended up in Honeysuckle house.

Mary asked how long Edith had been here. Where had she lived before? Were the staff decent? What was the food like? Did she ever get to leave the place and go out anywhere? Edith answered the questions in a monosyllabic monotone. What did Mary really want?

Mary seemed decent enough. She smiled and leaned forward in a friendly manner. Deciding to bring things to a head Edith asked, 'So, how did you know my Les?'

Mary looked out of the window for a couple of minutes before telling Edith that she had actually only met him once. She had worked as a barmaid at the Old Mo for one night only. Was supposed to be covering someone's week's holiday but got sacked after the first night. Earlier that evening she had watched him play darts with his mates. Noticed he disappeared and his team couldn't find him. By chance she had found him crouched on the floor in the corner of the cellar. Next to a beer barrel. Crying.

Edith raised both her eyebrows. 'I never knew …' she stammered.

It took Mary ages to find out what was his problem. He kept saying that no-one knew who he really was. Everyone would turn against him … Mary decided to open her heart to this vulnerable bloke. Something about him made her relate to him. She confided to Les that she was living with a woman. Rowena. A love-type thing. But they pretended to be sisters who hadn't managed to catch a husband. Shortage of men after the war and all that. No-one knew who she really was either. And on top of that she was a CO. That's why she had moved here from Sheffield. Asked Les not to hate her as she knew he had done his bit. … It was good to talk…

'But why the crying and the hiding?' asked Edith.

After lots of false starts Les had explained the situation. Felt that Mary would understand. It turned out that Les was going through the change. Had unexpectedly started a heavy period in the middle of the darts match. Soaked his trousers with blood. Couldn't walk across the pub like this. Had no idea what to do.

Edith gasped and put her hand across her mouth.

Mary's sister lived on the next road. Shaking her head and muttering to herself she sneaked out of the pub. Gone to her sister's house and asked to borrow a pair of her husband's trousers. Made up some daft sort of excuse. Just handed them to Les without a word and went back up to the bar. Returned to find queues of drinkers lined up, needing re-fills. The other barmaid was enraged and that was the end of her job. She and Les never spoke again.

Once, when she was walking down King's Heath High Street, she had seen Les and Edith walking along hand-in-hand on the opposite side. Looking happy. Thought about calling out to him. Realised it would just embarrass him. Wouldn't want to be reminded of that awful night. Would have loved to have gone over and told him Rowena had died. So few people who would understand what she was going through … And then this blasted stroke. No choice but to have carers in.

Edith was open-mouthed. She had no idea this had happened to Les. He would have kept it to himself to preserve his pride, she guessed. Such a dignified bloke. Felt so sad that he had gone through this. It made her question how else he had suffered. They had lived so many years together as man and wife that she didn't really think about it. Poor Les. Thank God, for Mary.

Having Les in common, they spent a lot of time together. Bonded. Not always talking about Les. They were strong women who fell in love with other women, and showed the courage to live as they wanted. Secretly. Edith kept the time of Les's funeral a secret. When his identity was discovered, some people started to gossip. She didn't want them to watch his burial out of curiosity. So only she, and Philip from the darts team attended.

Mary did battle with Rowena's family about her funeral. They were her legal relatives and hated Mary. Suspected their relationship was 'perverted' although never actually spoke about it. Believed she had corrupted Rowena and lead her into sin. They said they wanted to burial to be decent. In contrast to her life. Refused to allow Mary to attend. Mary explained to Edith how she watched from behind the fence. Saw Rowena's coffin being lowered. Knowing that Rowena loved her more than any of the relatives present. Only went to the grave-side after that miserable lot left. Wept alone for the love of her life.

Afternoons found Mary and Edith side by side in the garden. Or in inglenook in the lounge. Mary enjoyed telling Edith about her life with Rowena. The day trips to the seaside on the train. Weston Super Mare. Or Rhyl. Fish and chips on the prom.

Paddling in the sea. Saw a fortune-teller on the pier. Muffling their laughter as Gypsy Lee told them both that it wasn't too late. They still might manage to catch a husband.

Once they were walking around the Lickey Hills, when they started to argue. Neither of them could remember what it was about later. But Rowena had been angry and undid her bracelet and threw it at Mary. A precious bracelet. Mary had bought it for her their first Christmas together. Rowena rarely took it off. As she threw it, a gust of wind blew it past Mary, into a bush at the edge of the lake. They could see it hanging there out of reach.

Immediately regretful, Rowena had craned her neck over the edge, trying to reach it as it hung from the branch, extended over the water. Realising that it was too far out, Mary had leaned behind her and started prodding it with a stick. But the edge was slippery and Rowena started to slip. To save herself she grabbed Mary. The two of them ended up in the lake, submerged to their waists. Mary said they had nearly wet themselves laughing, but managed to retrieve the bracelet.

Edith and Mary chuckled at this. The silly things that made up the happy memories. When Les and Edith had first moved in together, Les had told her that he hated eggs. Edith had been brought up to believe that eggs were essential for good health. So, on Sundays she always made Yorkshire puddings with their dinner. Les loved them, and had no idea that they had eggs hidden in them. Silly bugger, she had said. She'd pulled the wool over his eyes for fifty years. And her smile faded a little as she remembered he was gone. She leaned her head on Mary's shoulder. Just for a moment.

It was a shock to Edith to realise the six weeks was up. The carer was back and Mary was going home. She would be picked up the next morning. Without thinking, she reached over and squeezed Mary's hand. Looked around quickly to see if the carers had noticed. Dreaded them finding out she was a dyke. She once heard them laughing in the staff room. One of them said she would refuse to bath a patient if she was lesbian. They would enjoy it too much. Would rather leave them to stink.

'Oh, you are awful,' her friend had replied.

Mary was reluctant to go home. Had become attached to Edith in the last few weeks. Felt close to her. Decided that she would ask her carer to take her to visit Honeysuckle House once a week. Perhaps they could even arrange for a couple of carers to take them both out together for lunch. Or to the botanical gardens. The seaside?

'Soon spring will be here again,' said Mary.

Edith mulled this over. The friendship was important to her. But she frowned.

'I could never fall in love again, 'she whispered. 'Not after Les.'

Mary smiled and shook her head.

'Me neither,' said Mary. 'But I do want to get the most out of these last years.'

They laughed together about how their sex drives had vanished years ago. But they both appreciated a cuddle. And company. Someone to laugh with. Confide in. They both wanted to feel precious.

Edith nodded. The loneliness that had overwhelmed her since Les died, had lifted a little. She enjoyed Mary's company.

'There are lots of different kinds of love,' said Mary, slipping her hand up inside the arm of Edith's cardigan.

Edith punched her gently on the arm and sighed.